CU00657865

UAR

‾enew or return items by the date
⅂ your receipt

tsdirect.org/libraries

and   0300 123 4049

ɔr hearing   0300 123 4041
ɔaired

CAMBRIDGE
UNIVERSITY PRESS

CAMBRIDGE
UNIVERSITY PRESS

University Printing House, Cambridge CB2 8BS, United Kingdom

Published in the United States of America by Cambridge University Press, New York

Cambridge University Press is part of the University of Cambridge.

It furthers the University's mission by disseminating knowledge in the pursuit of education, learning and research at the highest international levels of excellence.

www.cambridge.org
Information on this title: www.cambridge.org/9781107671492

First published 2013
Reprinted 2016

J. M. Newsome has asserted her right to be identified as the Author of the Work in accordance with the Copyright, Designs and Patents Act 1988.

Printed in the United Kingdom by Hobbs the Printers Ltd

Typeset by Aptara Inc.
Map artwork by Malcolm Barnes

A catalogue record of this book is available from the British Library.

ISBN 978-1-107-671492 paperback

The author wishes to thank Sophia Atcha, Captain Justin McComb, Connie Jensen, Andrew P. Petch, Kate Williams and Stephen Wood for their unstinted professional help.

Contents

Characters

Anika Hakim: a sixteen-year-old schoolgirl living in Alexandria, Egypt

Zaphira Bakkal: Anika's basketball team mate, also sixteen

Gamal Hakim: Anika's twenty-one-year-old brother

Ahmed Bakkal: Zafira's twenty-three-year-old cousin

Malcolm Maritz: a South African yacht owner

Sayid El-Karimi: Maritz's business partner

Musaid Diab: works for Maritz

Nikos Drakopoulos: a Greek police officer

Netta Savaki: a Greek police officer

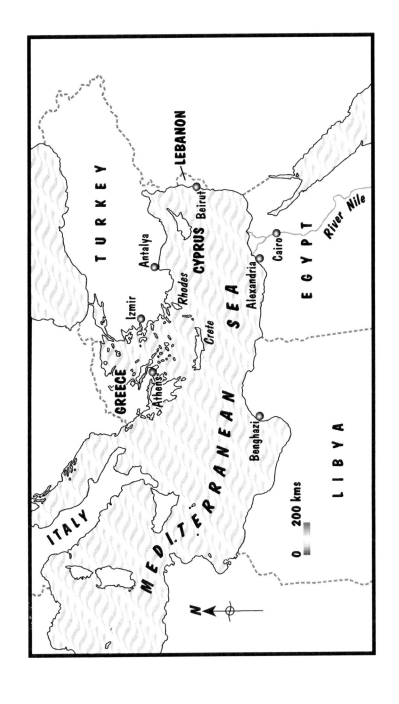

Chapter 1 *Explosion*

Anika could see that Zaphira was angry. 'What's wrong?' she asked.

'Your brother's late,' said Zaphira. She was looking round impatiently. Her wild brown hair was escaping from the knot she had tied it in for basketball training.

They were on the narrow finger of land in Alexandria that leads to Qaitbay Castle between the open sea and the East Harbour. They sat at a café table with glasses of orange juice and water on it. Even here by the sea, the evening was hot and still.

'I didn't know what time to say,' said Anika cheerfully. 'Our coach is never clear about what time we'll finish training, so ...' The look Zaphira gave her made her stop speaking.

The sea was very calm, and the sinking sun laid a fiery path across the dark water towards them.

Anika loosened her hijab a little and picked up her glass of juice. She looked around. Local people and foreign tourists were walking slowly up and down the open pedestrian area near the castle. Some, like Anika and Zaphira, sat at café tables which were set out here and there.

One couple were examining seashells laid out for sale on the pavement nearby. 'Look at this one, honey!' said the man in English. 'Look at the rainbow colours inside.'

Zaphira said in Arabic, 'Those shells don't even come from here.'

'Why don't you tell them?' Anika suggested with a smile.

'No point,' said Zaphira.

Anika wondered if Zaphira could speak English. The two girls had only met a few days before. Anika had recently moved up to the under-18s basketball team, and quite a few of the team-members were new to her.

Zaphira was tall. She played basketball aggressively and well, but she never seemed to smile. Anika, who always wanted everyone to be happy, had offered Zaphira a lift home. It was the day that Anika's youngest brother, Gamal, usually came for her in his car. On other days Anika's father sent his driver, which she found embarrassing.

She said, 'Hey, lighten up, Zaphira! I thought you'd like sitting here, near the castle, by the sea.'

'Your brother will never see us here.' Zaphira threw her arm out towards where the cars had to stop. 'We're a long way from where he can park.'

The few parked cars they could see were in front of a line of buildings which looked away from the open sea, onto Alexandria's East Harbour. Between the buildings Anika could see small boats and a few yachts in the harbour.

'I've met him here before,' said Anika. 'And he's not blind.' She took her cell phone out of her sports bag.

'Hmm!' Zaphira said, and drank some more orange juice.

Anika sent a text to Gamal. It said, 'Anything wrong? I'm at the usual table. Don't be long!'

Zaphira banged her glass down hard on the table and looked across the road, towards the buildings.

Anika thought, 'Maybe this was a mistake.'

She noticed a group of three men some distance away, in front of the large, solid building which was the Greek Maritime Club. One had a large moustache and the other two had their backs to her. One wore a backpack. Anika took a photo of them with her new phone. It was so easy. She took another and another.

'They'll see you,' warned Zaphira sharply. 'They'll think you're inviting them over. When your father is Umar Hakim, one of the richest men in Egypt, you need to be careful who your boyfriends are.'

'What?' Anika laughed. 'Don't be ridiculous!'

The smaller of the two men with their backs to the girls turned and stepped away from the others. He started to take off his backpack as he walked towards some parked cars.

Anika grinned, but quickly covered her mouth with her hand. She turned to Zaphira, her eyes shining. 'That's your cousin Ahmed, isn't it? I was wondering why he didn't come to watch us at training today, like he did last time. Who's he with?'

'Goodness knows,' said Zaphira. 'Friends, I suppose.'

Anika took some more photos. She hoped Ahmed would notice her, although she knew she didn't look her best straight after training. But he kept walking towards the cars.

She looked at the pictures she'd taken. The phone was expensive, a birthday gift from her father, and the photos were brilliant. Ahmed looked so handsome and fierce.

'Want to see?' she asked Zaphira.

Zaphira hardly looked. She sighed and said, 'If your brother's going to be any longer, I'll just have to get a bus.'

Anika put the phone away and went back to searching Qaitbay Road for her brother's car.

The man with the moustache was shouting at Ahmed. But Ahmed took no notice as he walked fast across the pedestrian area towards the girls. The other man had disappeared. Ahmed no longer had his backpack.

Anika hoped Ahmed was coming over to chat while they waited, but he kept looking over his shoulder, not at them.

A tall man with a large stomach came out of the Greek Maritime Club and walked towards a silver Mercedes. He was with a smaller man. They opened the doors of the car. Ahmed began to run. But he suddenly saw the girls in front of him and stopped dead with his mouth open in horror.

Then he raced up to them and grabbed Zaphira by the arm. 'Come with me. Now!' he shouted. 'It's not safe!' He caught Anika's hand as well, and pulled them both along beside the sea wall.

Zaphira actually smiled a little as she grabbed her purple sports bag and allowed Ahmed to pull her away.

'Hey! What are you doing?' she said. 'What's not safe?'

'Stop, Ahmed!' Anika laughed, picking up her own bag as she felt herself forced to run. 'Where are we going?'

Suddenly they were knocked to the ground as if they had been kicked from behind.

BOOOOOM-BOOOOOM! A long, deafening roar filled the air.

Pieces of pavement, car and café furniture fell around them, crashing onto the ground and into the sea. The noise echoed on and on. They could hear people screaming and shouting.

Ahmed jumped up and grabbed hold of them again.

'Come ON!' he shouted. Something hit Anika on her shoulder. She cried out, but Ahmed did not let go.

'Get UP!' he shouted. 'We can't stay here!' He dragged the two girls with him over a low wall and round behind a large, run-down building. There was a wide empty space beyond. Ahmed ran across it very fast, holding their arms so tightly that the girls could not escape from him.

They came to a fence. Ahmed pulled the girls through a broken gate into an open space with a small hut in it.

He paused for a moment. 'What in heaven's name am I going to do with you?' he cried with a worried frown.

They could hear police cars and ambulances arriving, their sirens going. Scared and injured people were shouting.

Ahmed looked around like a wild animal in a trap. He pushed them into the hut. 'Stay here!' he shouted at them. There was a pistol on a shelf by the door. Ahmed grabbed it. 'I have to get my mother,' he said desperately. 'Then I'll come back and get you.' He looked at Anika as if he wanted to say something else. Then he ran out with the pistol in his hand.

Zaphira jumped towards the door, but it shut in her face. 'Wait!' she shouted. 'What's going on?' They heard a wooden bar forced into place across the door.

Zaphira beat hard on the door, but it didn't move. The girls heard a loud cry of pain nearby, and then a shot. Zaphira shook the door uselessly again. Then she turned to Anika, her worried face full of anger and confusion.

Anika was sitting on the floor of the hut. Blood was spreading from her shoulder all down her white blouse.

Chapter 2   *Wounded*

It suddenly seemed quiet in the hut. There was a smell of old potatoes, and the air inside was hot and still.

'You're bleeding,' said Zaphira.

'Yes,' said Anika. 'Bit of a mess …'

'Let me see.' Zaphira knelt down behind Anika to take a look. She gasped quietly.

Anika said, 'I can hardly move my left arm, and my shoulder hurts a lot – at the back.'

Zaphira said, 'You've been hit by a sharp piece of metal.'

'Something fell on me as we ran,' said Anika. She felt gently with her right hand. There was something hard sticking out of her back. It hurt terribly. 'In God's name, what's that?' she asked in horror.

Zaphira found a clean pair of socks in her sports bag, opened her drinking bottle and poured the remaining water onto one of the socks. With one hand she took hold of the piece of metal sticking out of Anika's shoulder. 'Hold still,' she said, and pulled the metal out with one quick movement.

'Ow!' cried Anika. 'What …?'

Zaphira dropped the piece of metal on the ground and pressed the wet sock against the wound. The sock began to change colour from white to red.

'Ayayai! You're hurting me,' gasped Anika. 'Stop it!'

'You have a nasty, deep cut,' said Zaphira. She looked briefly under the sock. 'You're going to bleed quite a lot. Give me your other hand.'

Anika leaned away from Zaphira. 'Why?!'

'I want you to hold the sock against the cut to stop the bleeding.'

The pain was suddenly worse. It took Anika's breath away. She let Zaphira guide her hand to hold the sock in place.

'Push as hard as you can,' said Zaphira. 'And breathe!'

Anika took a deep breath. 'That's a bit better. Thank you. It really hurts.' Blood began to show between her fingers.

The two girls were quiet for a few seconds. Anika was dealing with the pain. Zaphira listened carefully. The noises outside were still loud, but nothing sounded very close by.

'Are you sure we can't get out?' asked Anika.

'Yes, I'm sure,' Zaphira answered.

'It was another bomb, wasn't it?' said Anika quietly.

'Must have been,' said Zaphira through her teeth.

'Do you think Ahmed had something to do with it?'

'Must have. He doesn't usually lock his relatives in smelly old huts.'

'But why?' asked Anika. 'Why would he set off a bomb?'

Zaphira walked up and down. 'I don't know. And I don't know why he would run off with a gun.'

'Zaphira, we have to get out of here!' Anika cried. She tried to stand up.

'Stay there,' said Zaphira. 'I'll text for help,' and she got her phone out of her bag.

Anika suddenly remembered. 'I took photos of them!'

Zaphira swore loudly. 'I'd forgotten that. Stupid of me! Where's your phone now?' she asked urgently.

Anika dropped the bloody sock and took out her phone.

Zaphira put her own phone in her pocket and looked around the hut. 'We have to hide your phone somewhere,' she said. 'Ahmed may come back any second. The first thing he'll want is our phones.' The floor was hard earth. A few bricks were piled up in one corner. The one window, opposite the door, had metal bars and no glass. The hut was old, but the wooden walls seemed strong.

'Don't hide it!' begged Anika. 'I need it with me. I could just delete the photos …'

'No!' Zaphira almost shouted, her eyes wide. 'If ever we get out of this, we may need those photos.'

Anika was trying to switch her phone on. Her hand was covered in blood. 'We didn't actually see Ahmed plant the bomb,' she said. 'Maybe the photos show who really planted it.' She shook the phone. 'It's dead! It won't work!' Her voice rose in panic. 'What's wrong with it?'

'Maybe it broke when you fell,' whispered Zaphira.

'But …' Anika banged the phone on her leg. 'Oh, dear God! How will anyone find us?'

'I'll send a text to my mum from my phone in a minute,' said Zaphira. 'We'd better hide yours anyway. Even if it's broken, someone might be able to get at those photos.'

'But this cost … I don't know … a lot.'

'I know!' whispered Zaphira fiercely. 'But if Ahmed did plant that bomb, he'll think we saw him and he'll need to silence us. Give it to me. Please.'

Anika was shocked. 'You mean kill us? Ahmed?'

'Perhaps. Or keep us locked up, like in here. Please. Just give me the phone!' She leant over and took it from Anika's hand. Then she pushed the phone carefully between two bricks. Her hair had come loose now and fell across her face. When she turned back, there was no sign of the phone. 'How is the wound?' she asked Anika.

'Very sore,' Anika said. The pain came and went in waves. 'Please ask someone to come and get us out. Please!'

'OK, OK,' said Zaphira, texting from her own phone.

Anika rocked backwards and forwards on the floor. 'Why has he locked us up?' she whispered to herself.

Zaphira sent her message. 'I think Ahmed has another choice,' she said thoughtfully. 'He could beat us to death, then take our bodies and leave them near the explosion. That way our families will think we'd been killed by the bomb.'

Tears ran down Anika's cheeks and she rocked faster. 'I don't know him. I've never spoken to him. He wouldn't do that, would he? Oh, I just can't think!'

'You're wounded and in shock.' Zaphira was matter-of-fact. She was walking backwards and forwards. 'If Ahmed comes back – alone or with someone else – we may have to fight. The quickest thing is to kick them between their legs.'

'No!' gasped Anika, shaking her head.

'Or you can hit them across the throat with the side of your hand, like this.' She showed Anika how to hit the voice box in the neck. Anika sat still, her mouth open in horror. She was thinking, 'This can't be true. I'm having a bad dream. It's all that street violence we've had in Egypt these last few months.' She tried again to get up. 'I can't stand up!' she whispered in panic. 'I'm so dizzy. My head's going round and round.'

But Zaphira was still talking. 'You need to keep your head down – and don't fall over. They can easily kick you to death if you're on the floor.'

Just then a step sounded at the door and someone pulled the length of wood away.

Chapter 3 *In the hut*

The door was thrown open with a bang. A man stood for a second in the doorway, staring at them.

Then he said, 'Wow! Ahmed told me to stay away from the hut when I caught him just now. But he didn't say why.'

He was older than Ahmed, taller and broader. His large teeth stuck out over his bottom lip. His eyes went from Anika on the floor to Zaphira, who stared at him hard.

She said, 'Is Ahmed OK?'

The man didn't answer. He just said, 'You must be Zaphira, Ahmed's tall cousin. He told me about you last week – and your basketball team.' He looked back at Anika. 'What's the matter with her?'

'She's hurt. We need to get her to an ambulance. What have you done to Ahmed?'

'You'd better come with me,' said the man, ignoring her question. He pointed at the sports bags. 'What's in those?'

Zaphira didn't answer, so Anika said, 'Our training things.'

'And a cell phone or two?' he said. 'Come on. Give them to me. You won't be needing them now.'

Anika groaned and hid her face with her bloody right hand. She thought, 'He's not going to help. He's just a thief.'

Zaphira said, 'We can't find her phone. I've got mine here.' She moved towards the door. 'Thanks for letting us out.'

The man grabbed Zaphira's phone from her hand before she could stop him. He looked at the message she had just sent. 'Not helpful,' he said, looking at her with an ugly smile. And he began writing a new text on her phone.

'Stop it!' Zaphira shouted, and jumped at him. He hit her hard across the face. She fell to the floor with a cry. He finished sending his message as she got up, shaking her head to clear it, her hair flying. She jumped towards him again.

'Don't be even more stupid,' he said slowly. A small gun had appeared in his hand, pointing at Zaphira's chest. Anika gasped. He said, 'Your mother will stop worrying now, but it's time for you to start.' He looked down at Anika and then back to Zaphira. He didn't take his eyes off her face as he dropped her phone on the ground, stepped on it and turned his foot. The phone broke into tiny pieces.

He took another phone out of his pocket, flipped it open, and spoke into it. 'Found two females. Something to do with Ahmed. Bringing them to the crossroads. There in two minutes.' He dropped the phone back into his pocket.

'Get up!' he said to Anika.

Anika tried to stand.

'Help her!' he shouted at Zaphira.

Anika was shaking so much she could hardly breathe. Zaphira leant down to help her up.

The man smiled. 'So, Zaphira Bakkal, eh? The boss'll know what to do with you. How much do you know?'

Zaphira was suddenly still. 'Boss? What boss?' she asked.

The man laughed. 'You'll soon find out,' he said, and waved his gun at the door. 'Start walking!'

Zaphira's light brown eyes narrowed as she stared at him.

Then she put her arm under Anika's good arm and helped her towards the door. The noises outside were still loud and confused. It was getting dark.

Zaphira whispered in Anika's ear, 'Groan!'

Anika looked at her sideways, and groaned a little.

Zaphira went on, 'Pretend you're hurt even worse than you are. When I push you, fall down and roll away.'

Anika groaned again, this time for real.

They walked slowly out of the hut. Zaphira held Anika up as she dragged her feet.

'Move!' shouted the man from behind them. 'That way!'

Zaphira pushed Anika gently.

'Aagh!' Anika shouted and fell on her good shoulder. She rolled off to the right. The pain made her cry out again.

Zaphira immediately stepped back towards the man, bending low. As she reached him, she hit up at his arm with all her strength. The gun went off and then flew onto the roof of the hut.

Zaphira went for the man's neck, hitting his voice box with one hand, then between his legs with her knee. He fell down, unable to breathe. Zaphira stood over him.

'Give me your hijab!' she cried to Anika.

Anika unwound her hijab shakily, using her right hand. She couldn't believe what Zaphira had done.

Zaphira forced the man's hands behind his back and tied them with the hijab.

'Give me a reason to kick you again,' she said quietly through her teeth. 'I'd like that.' The man coughed and groaned.

Now that there was hope of escape, Anika found the strength to stand. Zaphira ran into the hut and got their bags and Anika's phone. She searched through the broken parts of her own phone and found the SIM card.

The man had his back to them and was trying to get up as Zaphira came out of the hut. She stepped over to him, pushed him down again and kicked him hard in the face with the back of her heel. There was a cracking sound. He screamed and lay still, blood running from his face. Zaphira put her hand into his pocket and took his phone.

Anika was horrified. This girl was a gangster!

Zaphira picked up her own bag, took Anika's as well, and grabbed Anika's good arm. She pulled her towards a broken-down wall, away from the way they had come.

'Did you kill him?' Anika asked as they ran.

'Broke his nose,' replied Zaphira shortly. 'He was with Ahmed earlier. I recognised him. If we can get through here onto the main road, we can get you to an ambulance.'

They ran out from between buildings onto Qaitbay Road, and stopped dead.

To their left, the whole of the front of the Greek Maritime Club was damaged and burning. The pedestrian area was covered with earth and lumps of pavement. There was a huge hole in the road full of fire. Orange flames and black smoke poured up into the darkening sky. There were people everywhere, some wandering around bleeding and confused, others running to help. Voices shouted, engines thundered. Blue and red lights from fire engines, ambulances and police cars flashed near the hole and along the main road. The last light from the sun was an angry red line above the sea.

'Perhaps Gamal is looking for us,' shouted Anika, searching the crowd for her brother's familiar face.

Chapter 4   *Swinging boat*

Two policemen were directing ambulances between stopped cars. The girls ran across the main road, avoiding the cars and the trees in the middle.

Anika was shaking all over. 'I'll have to stop,' she said to Zaphira. 'I can't …'

Zaphira helped her to sit on a low wall in front of a large building. 'Sit here a minute,' she said. An ambulance was coming towards them from the scene of the explosion.

Zaphira stepped forward and raised a hand to stop it, but the driver called out of his open window that his passenger was dying and he couldn't stop now. Zaphira stepped back. 'No sign of Gamal?' she asked Anika.

'I can't see his car,' said Anika, desperately looking for it.

Just then they saw the man from the hut appear further up the road. He was covered in blood and walking as if he couldn't see. Anika's hijab hung from one wrist. He shouted to the policemen about two dangerous women.

Zaphira grabbed Anika's good hand and pulled her up and round a corner. 'We have to hide until he's gone,' she said as they ran down a narrow street towards the harbour.

Anika was feeling very strange, as though her feet were not touching the ground. She seemed to be flying in a fog, and she began to laugh.

The street ended on the sand. There were boats pulled up in rows and others in the water. Anika was laughing, but she was also shaking violently.

Zaphira looked around. All the boats were open and most of them were old. One, tied up to a wooden walkway nearby, looked new and clean. It was white, with a black cover over the back.

'Here,' Zaphira said, and pulled Anika towards it.

The boat rocked on the water as they climbed in. Zaphira pulled the stiff black cover over them and their bags. 'Keep quiet and lie still,' she whispered fiercely. 'If you move the boat will move and he'll find us!'

Anika stopped laughing.

'Just breathe,' Zaphira said. 'In, out. In, out. Slowly.'

Anika felt that each time she breathed in, she rose in the air. It was quite pleasant, except she couldn't stop shaking.

Suddenly, someone jumped into the boat and made it rock. Zaphira swore under her breath. A man's voice groaned as something heavy was put down in the boat.

Anika lay on her side, her good arm around her knees. It was hot under the cover. She began to lift it up. Zaphira's hand grabbed her ankle and fingernails dug into her leg.

She gasped as a man's voice spoke – an Arabic voice, but speaking in English. 'Had some trouble. May have to kill them both. I'll need help in a minute.' And there was the click of a cell phone closing.

Anika froze. 'Kill them both?' she thought. 'Us?'

The engine started and the boat shook.

Anika felt Zaphira's hand squeeze hers in the dark. 'Can't mean us,' whispered Zaphira under the noise of the engine.

'She does understand English,' Anika thought.

The boat picked up speed, then almost immediately slowed down. Anika expected the man to pull back the cover at any moment.

The engine stopped and the boat bumped gently against something.

'Help me here!' called someone in English. The boat moved up and down as something heavy was lifted out of it. Then the boat was still. 'We're tied up to another boat,' thought Anika.

'In there,' said another man. He sounded a bit like a friend of her brother's from South Africa and he seemed very excited. 'Did you see it up close?' he asked.

'Yes,' said the first man. 'I took photos for you.'

'And did you send the message?' asked the South African.

'Of course,' said the first voice.

Zaphira's mouth was beside Anika's ear. 'I've got a knife in my bag,' she whispered. 'When they've gone, I'll cut the ropes tying the boats together. Then we'll take this boat and go back.' Anika sighed and squeezed Zaphira's hand.

The South African voice called, 'Boat chains!' and there was a new, metallic noise. Then it felt as if the boat was lifting into the air. Zaphira swore quietly.

The boat started to swing a little again, then settled.

The South African called, 'We're ready to leave! Everyone back to work! Tell Musaid to cover the boat.' His voice got excited again as he moved away. 'So, what did you see?'

Zaphira lifted a corner of the cover. The air was fresh, but there was almost no light now. A larger engine started up.

'Where in heaven's name are we?' whispered Anika.

'On a yacht,' said Zaphira.

'So no ropes to cut? No escape?'

'No,' said Zaphira.

'Oh God!' said Anika. 'We must tell them we're here. We can't just go out to sea! We need to get home.'

'I doubt they're going far,' said Zaphira.

She was taking the SIM card out of the phone she had taken from the man in the hut. 'Perhaps just along the coast.' She put her own SIM card into the phone. 'That man talked about killing people as if he does it every day. Someone like that won't be pleased to see us on his yacht.'

Anika pulled back more of the cover and looked out. Her eyes wouldn't focus. 'We have to jump off and swim!' she said, trying to stand up.

'Don't be stupid!' Zaphira grabbed Anika and pushed her back down into the boat. It swung alarmingly. 'You can't swim with that wound. You'll drown!'

'You go then, and get help! Please, Zaphira! We can't stay here,' Anika begged.

'No, I can't leave you here bleeding to death.'

'But these men are dangerous. You heard them.'

'They don't know we're here, and we can make sure they don't find out if you keep still,' replied Zaphira calmly. She was trying to turn the cell phone on, but it wouldn't work.

They heard a chain being pulled up at the front of the yacht.

Zaphira lifted the cover right back. 'They've gone,' she said. 'And this is a really big yacht. These men must be rolling in money.'

Anika felt as if she were falling. She lay down in the bottom of the boat, trying to focus her eyes. Her shoulder was burning with pain, and she was very thirsty. 'You're crazy, Zaphira,' she said. 'How are we going to get back? Are you planning to take over the yacht?'

'Depends!' Zaphira raised her shoulders and half-smiled.

Anika took a breath to argue, but Zaphira whispered, 'Not now, anyway. You're in a bad way, and we both need a safe place to hide – and water to drink. I'll be back soon.' And she disappeared, setting the boat swinging again.

When the swinging stopped, Anika risked sitting up and looking around. She was sitting in a boat which was hanging above a wide, open space at the back of a huge yacht. She could see a door into the covered part of the yacht where the cabins must be. Everything was painted white.

'I am completely alone,' she thought, 'with a bleeding hole in my shoulder and a wild gangster girl, on a yacht that probably belongs to criminals.' She took a shaky breath. What should she do? What would her grandmother do?

'Never get into such a situation in the first place,' she answered herself. 'Bloody Zaphira! She got me into this.' All Anika wanted was for the pain to be less and the world to keep still. She imagined being with her grandmother at home. Grandma would bandage the wound and talk quietly about her childhood among the fields by the Nile, and Anika would feel calm and safe again.

But she wasn't at home. The engine was making the sea behind the yacht boil, leaving a long pale line on the dark surface. The city lights, like rows of stars, were growing fainter. Zaphira had been wrong: they were heading straight out to sea, not along the shining, friendly coast.

A sudden, horrifying thought came into Anika's mind. 'What has happened to Gamal? Was he there when the bomb went off?' She bit her lip and stopped breathing. Her stomach tightened in fear. Everything went black as she passed out.

Seconds later she came to, lying on the bottom of the boat, staring at the stars in the sky. She smiled at their beauty.

And then the pain and fear came back and she remembered what had happened.

'I mustn't panic,' she thought. 'It won't help Gamal. I must think. If only my shoulder hurt less …' But the questions kept going round and round in her mind. Was Gamal OK? If he was, was he looking for her? What made Zaphira so violent? 'I believe she's enjoying herself,' she thought. 'No wonder she's such a scary basketball player.'

The questions kept coming. How was Ahmed involved? If he *was* the bomber, why had he done it? What would her family be thinking now? How could she tell them she was still alive?

'But I might not be soon,' she thought suddenly, her heart racing. 'Supposing someone does come to cover the boat. Oh God, what shall I do? What would Dad do?'

She tried sitting up again. The pain was bad and she felt strange, but the dizziness was less.

'I shall ask the men to take us back,' she decided at last. 'We're not a danger to them. We're just two girls, frightened by the bomb. How could we threaten them?'

She looked over the side of the boat. It hung about two metres above the deck of the yacht. It wasn't far to jump and the engine noise would cover any sounds she made.

Suddenly the boat rocked. Anika's heart stopped. She turned and saw Zaphira climbing in from the other side.

'How did you get here without my seeing you?' she said. 'You frightened the life out of me!'

'Sorry,' whispered Zaphira. She picked up both bags from the bottom of the boat. 'I've found us a good place to hide.'

Chapter 5 *A safe place*

'Put your jacket on and come with me,' Zaphira added. 'Can you climb out?'

'You go ahead. I'll manage.'

The boat swung wildly as the girls climbed down. Anika followed Zaphira through the door she had noticed earlier into a corridor. The walls were white and the floor was covered with thick, blue carpet. Immediately on their left was a staircase going down. Beyond the staircase there were two doors on the left and three on the right. Zaphira led Anika past the stairs, towards a cloudy glass door at the end of the corridor. It seemed to lead to a kind of sitting room or salon, because it sounded as though there were people in there having a good time. Anika's heartbeat was so strong, she could hardly breathe.

Zaphira led her to the second door on the right and they went into a large dark cabin. It was richly furnished, with a big bed, armchairs, cupboards and drawers. There was a huge mirror opposite the bed, and a window looking out across the narrow deck at the passing water. The window had long curtains on each side. A little light came from outside, but more came from a green sign over the door saying EXIT. A shiny rail ran all round the walls at waist height.

Zaphira turned the key in the lock. 'We'll be fine in here,' she whispered. 'But don't switch the lights on, OK?'

'I'm not stupid,' Anika whispered back as she sat on the bed. It was very soft. Her head felt so light she thought she would rise to the ceiling and hang there like a balloon. She looked at Zaphira as steadily as she could. 'Why don't we just tell them we're here?'

'No chance,' said Zaphira. 'We need to know more about them before we do that.' She went over to a smaller door and opened it with a smile. 'Look at this!'

Anika took a deep breath and went to see. Beyond the door there was a luxurious bathroom, lit only by an emergency light. 'Oh, wow!' she gasped. 'Soft bed, private bathroom … Are you sure no one will try and use this cabin?' she whispered.

Zaphira didn't reply. She began to help Anika off with her jacket and blouse. 'We need to clean you up – and find something to drink.'

'What about the bruise on your face?' said Anika, undoing her buttons with her right hand. 'It's gone black.'

'That's just the light in here,' said Zaphira. 'Anyway, there's not much you can do about a bruise.' She was still trying to help Anika.

'The water in the taps may not be clean enough to drink,' said Anika, pushing Zaphira's hands away. 'You find us some drinking water. I can manage.'

Zaphira looked surprised and a little hurt, but she went back into the bedroom, and quietly started opening and closing cupboard doors.

Anika managed to get her blouse off and wet a towel with water from the tap. She couldn't see her wound very well, but she managed to wash away a lot of blood. It too was black in the strange green light. It made her think of Gamal. Was he lying somewhere covered in blood? 'Mustn't think about that!' she told herself.

Zaphira came into the bathroom with a bottle of water.

'I found this in a cupboard. Have a drink,' she whispered.

'Thanks,' said Anika, and drank. 'That was very good,' she said, handing the bottle back.

'You have blood all down your back, and in your hair, too,' said Zaphira. 'Shall I clean it off?'

'Yes,' said Anika. 'Please.' She turned round and watched in the bathroom mirror as Zaphira ran the tap quietly and gently cleaned away the blood.

Anika asked her again, 'Won't they want this cabin?'

Zaphira whispered, 'When I was looking around earlier, I only found signs of three men and the captain, though there must be others who work for them on the yacht. There are five bedrooms on this deck, and three of them are locked. The captain seems to sleep in the pilot house on the top deck.'

'So who's in the room behind the glass door?' asked Anika.

'It sounded like the two men we heard earlier,' said Zaphira. 'And there was someone in the kitchen, so I haven't been able to get us anything to eat yet.' Zaphira took another towel and dried Anika's back. 'You're still bleeding,' she whispered. 'We should at least tie your hair up and cover the cut.'

Anika shook her head. She pulled a towel round her shoulders. 'Not now. I'll just wear this. What can we cover it with, anyway? And I want to wash my blouse.'

Sound burst into the corridor, making them jump. The glass door must have opened and the girls heard someone walk past their door towards the back of the yacht. There must have been a television in the room beyond the glass door, because they could now hear a loud voice speaking in English. It sounded like a newsreader. Zaphira left the bathroom and made a sign to Anika to come and listen. They stood side by side, ears to the cabin door.

They heard '… Minister of Transport, and Mr Mostafa Wahab, the Harbourmaster of the Alexandrian Port Authority, were both killed instantly. So far, there are another four people dead and thirty-two injured. The Minister of Transport had been a guest of Mr Wahab at the Greek Maritime Club. Witnesses told us that Mr Wahab often spent time there. The bomb was under Mr Wahab's car. The number of dead and injured is expected to rise, the police say. We understand that the Democratic Freedom Party, the DFP, has said it is responsible for the explosion. They say it is "an attack on our new gangster Government – a government that promised the Earth, but has not listened to the people of our beloved country". The chief of police is with me now. So, is it true, sir, that the bomb was planted by the DFP? They have no history of such …'

The glass door banged shut and the girls couldn't hear the television clearly any more.

They looked at each other in shock.

Anika sank on to the bed with a groan.

'I can't believe Ahmed planted that bomb,' she whispered. 'Maybe he knew about it, but he looks too nice to do anything like that, whatever his politics.'

Zaphira sat beside her. 'Perhaps someone offered him a lot of money,' she suggested.

Anika jumped up and turned on her. 'You really are crazy, aren't you?' she whispered fiercely, tears in her eyes. 'How can you think that, about your own cousin, that he would kill people for money? You think the worst of everyone! You crash your way through life like you do on the basketball court. You positively love violence. And you think it solves all problems, don't you?'

Zaphira stood up in surprise. She was taller than Anika and looked down at her calmly. 'You are partly right,' she said slowly. 'I don't trust anyone, not even my family. I've learned that the hard way. But I do *not* think violence solves all problems. And I don't *enjoy* it. I'm just …' She paused, then said, 'I'm just used to it. And clearly, you … are not.'

Anika looked at Zaphira in horror, and sat down on the bed again. Her heartbeat was shaking her whole body and the pain in her shoulder was like a knife. She pulled the towel closer. It was dark with blood.

Zaphira got another towel from the bathroom and laid it on the bed. She signed to Anika to lie on it. Anika just looked at her.

Zaphira lifted her shoulders. 'OK,' she whispered. 'Suit yourself. I can't hear much movement out there now, so I'll go and see if I can get some food.' She opened the door, looked both ways along the corridor and left, closing the door quietly behind her.

To Anika the walls and floor seemed to be moving in a wind, like curtains by an open window. She lay down on the towel on the bed, and shut her eyes.

Chapter 6 *Visitor*

When she opened her eyes again, Zaphira was sitting on the side of the bed, eating bread and cheese. It was still dark outside, and there was loud music playing somewhere.

'You've been asleep,' whispered Zaphira. 'Want some food?'

Anika nodded. She was surprised that Zaphira didn't seem to be upset with her.

They ate in silence.

'That was good,' Anika said at last. 'Thank you.' She had no appetite, but she'd drunk a whole carton of orange juice.

'You're welcome,' said Zaphira. 'I've washed your blouse and had a shower. Do you want one?'

'That would be good,' Anika said.

'Can you manage on your own?'

'I think so,' said Anika, as she stood up carefully.

Later, showered and dressed again in her basketball shirt, Anika sat on the bed. Zaphira was sitting on the other side, leaning against the pillows with a sheet over her. She had the man in the hut's cell phone in her hands.

She said, 'I thought I could get this to work. No luck.'

'That's a pity,' said Anika. She took a notebook and pencil out of her sports bag. 'How's your bruise?'

'Forgotten about it,' whispered Zaphira. 'Is that a diary?'

'No. I … just like to have a notebook to draw in …' She turned her back and wrote on a plain page, 'Who is the real Ahmed?' in her best Arabic script. Then she added fine lines until she had hidden the words among the leaves of a beautiful tree. Her wounded shoulder ached as she worked. 'Thank goodness I'm right-handed,' she thought.

After a while, Zaphira said, 'Is *your* phone working?'

'No,' said Anika, closing the notebook. She got into the huge bed. There was more than a metre between the two girls. 'It's dead,' she added, speaking to Zaphira in the mirror opposite.

'Probably a good thing,' said Zaphira. 'Better that we keep those photos you took of Ahmed a secret – at least for now.'

'I don't believe he did it!' Anika whispered fiercely. 'We didn't actually see. It could have been one of the other guys.'

'He knew there was a bomb. That's why he pulled us away.'

'That doesn't mean he planted it.'

Zaphira looked sadly at Anika. 'You're not being logical,' she said, and turned away to look out at the dark waves.

Anika's watch said 00.34. The music suddenly stopped and the glass door opened and shut. Unsteady feet sounded in the corridor. Doors shut and a key turned.

Zaphira whispered, 'Sounds like they're going to bed. Have you any idea where we might be going?'

Anika sighed shakily. 'How should I know?' she answered. 'Wherever it is, it's too far away from home.' She felt tears on her face and rubbed them away with her towel.

'Chose the wrong boat, didn't I?' whispered Zaphira.

Anika looked at her in the mirror in surprise. She nodded, and then hid her face in the towel.

Zaphira looked straight at Anika in the mirror, with her head on one side. 'Shall I go and murder them in their beds?' she whispered with a slight smile. 'Then we can turn the yacht round and go home.'

Anika suddenly felt completely exhausted. She lay down and closed her eyes. 'You really are crazy,' she said. 'You don't need to kill people to do what's right.'

'Don't be so sure,' Zaphira said quietly to the passing sea.

*   *   *

Anika woke to the sound of their cabin door handle being shaken. It was daylight, and a man was swearing in Arabic as he tried to get in.

Anika reached over and grabbed Zaphira's arm. She whispered, 'Quick! Hide!'

Zaphira was up and in the bathroom before Anika had got out of bed. She came out again quickly with all the wet and bloody towels and pushed them into a cupboard in the bedroom. Then she grabbed Anika's blouse and their sports bags and hid them in another cupboard.

The door stopped shaking. They heard the man swearing again as he went away.

The rising sun shone in through the window. The waves were larger than in the night. The yacht rose and fell more.

'Did you hear?' whispered Anika. 'He spoke in Arabic. Everyone else on this boat talks in English.'

'He may be OK,' said Zaphira. 'But we'd better be sure. We'll hide behind the curtains if he comes back.'

They made the bed and smoothed out the covers. Zaphira took the key out of the door. They stood still, one on each side of the window, beside the curtains, waiting.

They listened to the engine and the sound of the water along the sides of the yacht. They noticed for the first time the pattern of grey leaves on the pink wallpaper which matched the thick grey carpet.

They waited. Anika's watch said 07.32.

Just as they were beginning to relax, the door shook again as someone unlocked it. They jumped behind the curtains and held their breath.

They heard someone come in and go into the bathroom.

It was a man, and he was talking to himself in Arabic. 'No taps running here,' he said quietly. He came back into the bedroom. 'And none anywhere else. So why is the fresh water level going down so fast?'

The girls heard him sigh. 'And why,' he said sadly to himself, 'was this room locked? I never lock the empty rooms. It's a good thing we keep spare keys. Must be going mad. Mad Musaid …'

And he let himself out, leaving the door unlocked.

Zaphira went very quietly to the door and listened. Then she put her key in the lock and turned it.

The two girls looked at each other across the room. The man had sounded so confused and sad that they broke out in silent laughter at him.

But their laughter didn't last long. They sat down well away from the window and spoke in whispers.

'What are we going to do?' asked Anika.

Zaphira said, 'We only have two choices: tell someone we're here, or keep on hiding.'

'If we tell them we're here …' began Anika.

'We might get thrown into the sea, dead or alive,' Zaphira finished her sentence for her. 'Or be locked up till we get to a port and handed over to the police. Or sold back to our families. Hmm! Not much chance with mine,' she added with a hard little smile.

'Or,' said Anika, 'they might help us get a message home.'

'Mmm. More likely tie us up and rape us.'

'Where do you get these ideas?' Anika asked in disbelief.

'These things happen where I live,' said Zaphira shortly.

Anika realised how lucky her own family had been in the recent political unrest. She said, 'Is that why you learned to fight?'

'My brother went to *taekwondo* lessons before he was killed. He used to come home and teach me so that he could practise with me.'

'Your brother was killed?' Anika was shocked.

'Yeah,' Zaphira said shortly. Then she sighed. 'He was in the wrong place at the wrong time, like our dad. There are no men in my family now, and I'm the eldest girl.'

'I didn't know,' said Anika. 'I'm so sorry.'

She thought again about what might have happened to Gamal. She sat with her hand over her mouth and tears in her eyes, unable to speak.

Zaphira was looking out at the moving sea. 'You know, I've never been to sea before.'

Anika took a deep breath. 'Really!' she whispered. 'You seemed to know all about boats when you were exploring the yacht earlier.'

'It's a weird feeling, isn't it? When nothing stays still.'

'A bit like life in Egypt this year,' said Anika.

Zaphira turned to her. 'I think we should stay hidden. We might be discovered, of course, but if not, we'll escape when we get to land, and ask the police to send a message home.'

'That could be in Turkey or Greece,' said Anika.

'Or Italy,' whispered Zaphira.

'Or France.' Anika couldn't remember her geography. Her head felt as though it was full of bean soup.

'They all have police forces where someone is bound to speak English,' Zaphira said. She stood up. 'Perhaps I should see if I can find some more food.'

She went over to the door to listen. But instead of opening it, she bent down and picked something up off the floor. When she turned back to Anika, she was holding a piece of paper in her hand.

Chapter 7 *Phone calls*

'What is it?' whispered Anika in alarm. She went to see.

Zaphira opened the paper. 'It's a note,' she said quietly. 'In Arabic.' And she read, 'I know you are here. I smelled you. Perhaps you are the missing daughter of Umar Hakim, the businessman? Do you need some help? I haven't told anyone about you.' Zaphira looked up. 'And he has signed it: Mad Musaid.'

Anika took the note from Zaphira and read it again. 'How does he know I'm missing?' she whispered.

'He must have a radio or understand the TV,' answered Zaphira. 'Your family must have told the authorities.'

'I knew they'd be going crazy!' whispered Anika. 'I need to ask him about Gamal. I must tell him we do need help, and that I need to send my father a message to say I'm OK.'

'Don't do that,' said Zaphira. 'At least, not yet.'

'Oh please, don't start with the distrust business again,' said Anika. 'It's stupid to pretend we're not here any more. And Musaid obviously isn't going to hurt us. He has a key. He can come in any time he wants.'

'Maybe,' said Zaphira. She stood still. 'But you know what? There's a chance he doesn't know there are two of us.'

'What do you mean?' whispered Anika.

'It might be a good idea for me to stay hidden.'

'For goodness sake, Zaphira! You really are–'

Zaphira shook her head, her hair escaping from its knot. 'I'm not crazy, Anika. I'm just trying to keep you alive and safe.'

'Why?' asked Anika crossly. 'Why bother so much about me? I know from basketball that you think I'm pretty silly.'

Zaphira looked surprised. 'Not silly,' she said. 'Just … not very effective as a player.'

They heard a door open in the corridor, and the South African voice saying smoothly in English, 'What are you doing there, Musaid?'

Musaid answered close by, 'Just checking the towels in all the bathrooms, Mr Maritz, sir. May I check yours now?'

'Why not?' said Mr Maritz. 'Go ahead.'

Doors opened and shut and then there was silence.

'He was just outside the door!' whispered Zaphira.

Anika sat down on the bed. She was dizzy and shaking again. 'So now he knows there are two of us.'

'He may not have heard us. We were whispering, and the engine noise probably covered our voices.' Zaphira was taking Anika's bag out of the cupboard.

'What are you doing?' asked Anika.

'Looking for your phone.'

'It's in my left trainer,' whispered Anika. 'Under the inner sole.'

'Hey! You're learning!' said Zaphira, as she put the trainers back in Anika's bag. She went on, 'When Musaid comes again, I'll hide. And if he says anything, just say you were talking to yourself. OK?' She looked hard at Anika.

Anika shook her head and sighed. She rubbed her left arm gently with her right hand, and turned towards the window.

As she did so, a man walked past it, looking the other way at the dark blue sea. Anika dived behind the curtain. Zaphira, who was on her way into the bathroom, froze.

Anika could just hear the man's voice through the curtain and the cabin window. She recognised it. It was Mr Maritz! He seemed to have stopped close to their window and was talking in English on a cell phone.

'Thank you, Deputy Minister,' he was saying, his voice warm and smoothly polite. 'It is very good of you to deal with this on such a difficult day for you. The death of the Transport Minister is indeed a great shock, but of course you realise how good for your country my business will be. It will add greatly to the position of Alexandria airport as a centre of trade between southern Africa and Europe. … I'm very glad you agree. I will contact you again in two or three days. … Thank you again.'

There was a pause. He must have made a second call, and this time his voice was less attractive and much cooler.

'Good morning, Mr Bryant. … That's right. I am ready to make the arrangements now. … Yes, I heard about the bomb on television. … No, we'd already left. We didn't see anything. … Tomorrow would be best. … We can meet on my yacht. I'll be in the Flisvos Marina in Faliron. … Good. I'll expect you at eleven o'clock.' He moved away, still giving directions about where the yacht would be.

Anika carefully pushed the curtain aside.

'He's gone,' Zaphira whispered. 'He didn't look this way. So. That's Mr Maritz. Very handsome!' She went into the bathroom.

Anika thought, 'He might be handsome, but he's a liar. He said he didn't see the bomb explode yesterday because he was already at sea. But the yacht left after the bomb exploded. Why would he lie?' As she sat down on the bed, she thought, 'Maybe Zaphira's right. I'd better not try to talk to him. I might end up with *two* holes in me … And where on earth is Faliron?'

A few moments later Zaphira came out of the bathroom with her bag.

'You look awful,' she whispered to Anika. 'Shoulder bad?'

Anika looked up at her. 'Did you hear Mr Maritz? He said we'd arrive in Faliron by tomorrow morning, but I've no idea where that is.'

Zaphira pushed her bag into a cupboard. 'Tomorrow morning?' she said. 'Hmmm. So we just need to stay hidden till then. I'm pretty sure we'll find a way to escape once we're in a port.' She went to the door.

'What are you going to do?' asked Anika in alarm.

'I'll go and see if I can find us some more food,' Zaphira said. 'Breakfast coming up!' She locked the door behind her.

Anika stood up as quickly as she could, but it was too late. She was locked in.

Had Zaphira really gone for food? Was she perhaps looking for Musaid, or the 'handsome' Mr Maritz to make a deal? 'But what sort of deal could she make?' thought Anika. 'I mustn't start thinking like her. Dear God, how are we going to get back?'

Anika walked up and down, feeling more and more annoyed. It was better than feeling afraid.

Then she sat down in an armchair and opened her notebook. On a clean page at the back she began to put down what had happened to them so far in pictures and words, like a cartoon. Her hand hardly shook at all.

She was drawing herself in the empty cabin when she heard the key in the lock.

She was too far from the bathroom to hide. She shut the notebook and prepared herself for the worst.

But it was Zaphira again, with some very strange shapes in her tracksuit trousers. She closed and locked the door, and began to pull things out of her trousers – a loaf of bread, two cartons of orange juice, a cooked chicken leg, a piece of pizza, a small melon. Anika had to smile.

'I heard someone accusing Musaid in Arabic of stealing food,' Zaphira whispered seriously.

Anika sighed. 'I'm just hoping they don't find us,' she said. 'Thanks for the food. And is that juice?'

Zaphira handed Anika a carton of orange juice. 'Here,' she said. Then she looked at Anika with a slight frown. 'Are you all right? Turn round.'

Anika saw in the mirror that there was blood all down her back. No wonder she felt so dizzy.

Zaphira said, 'I found some bandages and painkillers in a cupboard in the kitchen. Let's get you cleaned up again.'

Zaphira cleaned Anika's wound and gave her two painkillers to take with the orange juice. Then she whispered, 'You'd better rest. Your skin feels hot. I think you've got a temperature.'

Anika lay back on the bed. To stop the horrors in her mind, she thought about her cartoon drawings. It would be good to draw Zaphira stealing from the kitchen …

Chapter 8 *Musaid*

When she woke, Anika looked beside the bed for her phone. Then she realised that of course she wasn't at home. No music, no checking up on friends on Facebook. She had been asleep for a while. The sun was much higher now.

Her watch said 12.30.

She sat up and saw that Zaphira was asleep in an armchair.

And Anika's notebook was open on her lap!

Anika got up as quietly as she could. Her shoulder hurt when she moved or took a deep breath. She gently lifted the notebook away from the sleeping girl's knees. The page was open at Anika's drawing of Ahmed's face.

She had done the drawing a few days before. It was the first time Ahmed had been to their training. He had stood quite still for a whole hour, watching her. Her body had felt new and strong, as though she had been given a superpower. She had told no one, but she had made this drawing so that she could remind herself of that feeling.

But now Zaphira had seen it, stolen her moment! She felt so angry and embarrassed that she sat down suddenly in the other armchair.

'Stupid, stupid, to leave the notebook out,' she told herself. 'Now she will think I'm even sillier than before.'

Zaphira stirred in her chair.

Anika thought, 'I feel so ill. And powerless! I must *do* something, or I shall go mad. I'll check my phone again.

If it won't work, I'll go and find Musaid to help me send a message.'

She stood up. But she had to sit down again. And even sitting down, she felt as though she were falling.

She tried once more to stand, but fell back into the chair again. Her heart was beating fast and she was breathless. She decided to keep the panic down by drawing a happy time. She started on a picture of her father and brothers playing football on a beach. But her hand shook too much and she had to give up.

She looked out of the window. From the short shadows she guessed they were travelling north-west. So where exactly was Faliron?

Beyond the glass door, she could hear two men's voices. It sounded as though they were speaking in English, but she couldn't hear any words. One voice was certainly Mr Maritz and the other sounded like the man they'd heard get into the small boat in Alexandria harbour.

Someone walked along the corridor past their cabin. It sounded as though they were carrying drinks with ice in, perhaps on a tray. The glass door opened and then shut again with the usual loud bang.

Zaphira woke up and jumped out of her chair, her eyes on the door.

'It's OK,' whispered Anika. 'I think they're having lunch.'

'No sign of Musaid?' asked Zaphira.

'Nothing.'

'You feeling better?'

'Can't stand up without falling over,' whispered Anika. 'But my appetite's come back.'

'Great. You have the chicken,' said Zaphira. She got her knife out, opened it, and cut into the melon.

As they were eating, Anika whispered innocently, 'What do you think of my drawings?'

'You made Ahmed too good-looking.' Zaphira spoke with her mouth full.

At that moment, a key turned in the lock and a man opened the door. Zaphira jumped up, ready to fight.

'My God!' said the man quietly in Arabic. 'There are two of you!' And he turned quickly to shut the door. 'How on earth did you get onto the yacht?'

Zaphira signed to Anika not to speak. 'Who are you?' she whispered.

'I left you a note,' the man whispered back. He was wearing a white uniform and had a large cloth bag in his hand. He was about Zaphira's height, with thick eyebrows and deep worry lines in his forehead. 'My name's Musaid. I work for Mr Maritz.'

'So what are you going to do?' Anika asked, ignoring Zaphira's instruction not to speak.

'It depends,' said Musaid. Then he noticed Anika's bandage. 'You're hurt!' He took a step towards her.

'Keep back!' warned Zaphira. 'What's in the bag?'

'Clean towels,' said Musaid, looking at Anika. 'I saw there weren't any before. You *are* Anika Hakim, aren't you?'

'You don't need to know our names,' said Zaphira.

'It's very important that I contact my family,' said Anika. 'Please could you help me to do that?'

'The television keeps saying that you're missing. You sent a message that you were at the café where the bomb went off, didn't you?' asked Musaid.

'No comment,' said Zaphira before Anika could answer.

'So you made no secret of being there,' said Musaid.

'So?' said Zaphira.

'So-o-o,' said Musaid, 'when they say on TV that Anika Hakim may have been the bomber – because she hasn't been found and she must have blown herself up with the bomb – they're probably wrong.'

'What!?' Zaphira stepped angrily towards him.

Anika couldn't move. She sat with her mouth open.

Musaid looked at them calmly. 'I thought so,' he said. 'The message you sent your brother about being late made that seem … unlikely. But that's what they're saying.'

'That's crazy!' breathed Anika at last. 'We had nothing to do with it.'

'Then why are you here?' whispered Musaid. 'If you didn't plant the bomb and run away, why didn't you just go home?'

Zaphira looked at Anika and then said, 'Well … a man we don't know threatened us. So we were afraid and we hid in a boat. That boat turned out to belong to this yacht.'

'I wondered why the cover was messed up,' said Musaid.

Zaphira went on, 'We didn't think anyone would actually use the boat.'

'You didn't think,' said Anika quietly.

'We – I – thought it was just tied up for the night,' Zaphira said. 'I thought we could hide in it till the man had gone.'

'Bad luck,' said Musaid. 'And now you will end up in Greece without papers.'

'Greece?' said Zaphira and Anika together.

'That's where we're going,' said Musaid. 'Faliron.'

The girls looked at each other.

Anika said, 'I've had enough of this. I want to tell Mr Maritz we're here and ask him to please help us contact our families. This whole thing is a ridiculous mistake.'

Zaphira shook her head. 'Don't be stupid!' she whispered.

'Telling Mr Maritz there are two young girls hiding on his yacht,' said Musaid, 'would be a very bad idea. He's a cruel and pitiless man.'

'I thought so,' said Zaphira. 'We'll just stay here quietly until we get to Greece.'

'But we have to tell our–' Anika was almost in tears.

'Listen,' said Musaid. 'I can't do anything just now, but I'll think about it. I'll just put these towels in the bathroom.'

'Put them here,' said Zaphira, pointing at the bed.

Musaid took the towels out of his bag and put them down on the bed. 'Try not to use so much water if you take another shower,' he said with a smile, and his anxious face changed completely. He looked kind and full of fun.

Zaphira said, 'OK. But we're going to need enough food and drinking water to keep us going until we get to … where did you say?'

'Faliron. It's on the coast, near Athens.'

'How long will that take?'

'We should be there by morning.'

'So will you help us with food and water?'

'I can try,' said Musaid. Then he smiled again, but with his head on one side. 'How will you thank me?'

Anika took a breath to ask what he meant, but Zaphira looked Musaid straight in the eyes and said, 'We'll find a way. You do right by us and we'll do right by you.'

Musaid looked back at Zaphira with one heavy eyebrow raised. 'Sounds good,' he said. Then he turned to Anika. 'Is there anything I can do for your shoulder?'

'Just some more clean bandages, if you have any,' she said.

'I'll see.'

'And let us know what's being said on the television,' said Zaphira. 'What's happened and who did plant the bomb.'

'And if my brother Gamal was injured or …' whispered Anika.

Musaid shook his head. 'Gamal Hakim looked fine to me,' he said. 'They showed him on TV reading out your last message, so he must be all right.'

'Really!' said Anika, and her eyes lit up. 'You saw him?'

Musaid said, 'Yes. Last night Mr Maritz watched the news again and again. Your brother was wearing a T-shirt with Alexandria University written on it. And glasses.'

'He needs them to read,' said Anika with a tearful grin.

'I'll come back with food and bandages later,' said Musaid.

He went out and they heard him lock the door.

'You see?' said Anika, still grinning. 'Being polite can get you what you need.'

'It depends who you're dealing with,' said Zaphira.

Anika got out her pencil and began a drawing of the sun coming up in the desert. Zaphira went back to her meal.

Chapter 9 *News*

It was after 3 p.m. when they heard the key in the door again. Zaphira went over to the door and waited where it would hide her as it opened. She had her knife in her hand. Anika stood up.

Musaid came in quickly and quietly – and alone. He turned to lock the door and saw Zaphira. She had already hidden the knife.

'I brought you these things,' he whispered, and dropped his cloth bag on the bed. 'Keep the room tidy as though you weren't here in case they look in. Hide in the bathroom if they do.'

'Thanks,' said Anika.

Musaid looked pointedly at Zaphira. 'I know someone with a small flat in Faliron. You can come there with me.'

'Right,' said Zaphira, holding his eyes with her own. 'If you come back, scratch on the door. Then we'll know it's you.'

Musaid nodded. 'No lights, no sounds,' he whispered as he left. His key turned in the lock.

Anika looked at Zaphira. 'Are you going to have sex with him?' she asked.

'Of course not!' Zaphira laughed.

'*He* thinks you are.'

'Naturally. That's what he's supposed to think.' Zaphira turned to the bag on the bed. 'Let's see what we've got here.'

The girls stood still as they heard someone walking past their door. The glass door in the corridor opened. And it stayed open. Beyond it, the television was very loud.

'… continues to cause concern,' said a woman's voice in English. 'But now we turn to the issue of who is responsible for the bomb. Back to you in the studio, Lee.'

'Thank you, Dawn. That was Dawn Walsh reporting from the scene of the Qaitbay Bomb, as it has come to be called. As you may have heard earlier, it was thought that Anika Hakim, who is still missing, may have been the bomber. Her father, businessman Umar Hakim, is believed to be a member of the DFP, the political party named in the message taking responsibility for the bomb.'

Anika, with her ear against the door, covered her mouth with her hand as she screamed silently. The announcer continued. 'However, the scene of the explosion has now been examined and this idea has been proved incorrect.

'Meanwhile, a sock with blood on it that may have been Anika's has been found on empty land near the scene. Also parts of a cell phone, possibly belonging to the girl she was with, who has not been named.'

Anika and Zaphira looked at each other, their eyes green from the light of the sign above the door.

'The police have just said that they think the message from the DFP is false. The DFP's head office denies all knowledge of the message and the bomb. Because of this and the sock, it is now thought that Anika and her friend may have seen something suspicious and been kidnapped by the real bomber.

'Anika is sixteen, with black hair and eyes. She was wearing a purple tracksuit and a black hijab. Her father and her grandmother appeared earlier on TV and begged viewers to help find her.

'Now to other news. In New York …'

The glass door closed with a bang. The girls heard footsteps pass in the corridor.

'Musaid must have left the door open so we could hear that,' whispered Zaphira.

Anika moved to the bed as if she were dreaming. She sat down by Musaid's bag. 'Poor poor Father,' she whispered to herself. 'And Grandma! Oh, dear God, why are you putting us all through this?'

Zaphira sounded bitter as she said, 'Your father is a clever man, with many sons and many friends. He even has relatives in this Government. He'll find out soon enough that Ahmed planted the bomb.'

'You can't be sure it was Ahmed!' Anika said.

'I think I can,' whispered Zaphira fiercely.

'Well, that doesn't change anything now.' Anika felt desperate. 'Or tell anyone where we are.' She stood up and walked backwards and forwards across the room as fast as she could. 'Why is this boat so slow!'

'Sit still!' said Zaphira. 'You'll open your wound again.'

Anika took a deep breath and came back to the bed. 'Musaid said he'd bring bandages.'

They opened the bag. There was bread and cheese, grapes, some honey cakes and bottles of water. In another package, there were bandages, painkillers, and two clean T-shirts.

'I'll put some of these bandages in your sports bag for later,' whispered Zaphira. 'Let's clean you up again. Then you must rest. You look exhausted.'

'And you're not, of course,' said Anika crossly.

'I don't have a hole in my shoulder that keeps bleeding,' said Zaphira. 'And the whole world isn't out looking for me because I'm the daughter of a well-known businessman and I may have witnessed a terrorist kill the Transport Minister.'

Anika looked away and lay down. The anger in Zaphira's face frightened her.

* * *

Anika woke at 17.32. The yacht was moving up and down a lot in the rough sea, and something was banging around in the cabin next door.

Zaphira was near the window, looking out.

'What's going on?' whispered Anika.

'Not sure,' Zaphira answered.

Anika got up and went to stand with Zaphira. At first there was nothing to see but the empty deck, the growing waves, and a lot of grey clouds building in the sky.

Then they heard someone running. They stepped back so as not to be seen. A man ran past. It was Ahmed!

And close behind him was a large man with a moustache and a pistol in his hand. He was shouting in Arabic. He jumped forward and caught Ahmed round the legs. Ahmed fell to the deck and lay still.

The girls watched in horror as the man with the gun pulled Ahmed past their window by his feet. His head left a line of blood on the deck. Spray from the waves began to wash it away.

Zaphira started towards their cabin door. Anika was nearer to it, and blocked her way.

'What are you going to do?' she whispered.

'Help Ahmed!' said Zaphira. 'Get out of my way!'

Anika stared at her and then stepped aside. 'OK,' she said. 'You go ahead and risk your life again. Perhaps you don't like your life very much. Perhaps you don't care whether you live or die. But I love my life.' She began to shake. 'My mother died when I was born so that I could live. I will not help you if you try to kill that man. I want Ahmed to be free, but …' She was shaking so much she had to sit on the bed.

Zaphira stood like a statue with her hand on the door handle. Then she moved stiffly to an armchair and sat down.

Anika's mind had stopped working. She sat rocking and staring at the carpet.

After a few moments, Zaphira said, 'Why is Ahmed here on Maritz's yacht? What has Maritz got to do with Ahmed?' She was silent for a while. Then she said, 'That man with the moustache was with Ahmed at Qaitbay yesterday. And now they're both here on this yacht with Maritz. But why?'

Then she jumped up. 'Of course! Maritz ordered the bomb! Ahmed and the man with the moustache are working for him! They were the ones on the boat with us when we were under the cover. Ahmed must have been unconscious.'

Anika shook her head. 'No!' she said.

Zaphira had to grab the wall-rail as the yacht rose and fell. 'The bomb killed the Minister of Transport and the Harbourmaster. Why would Maritz want them dead?'

The sky outside was now dark grey, and the yacht was beginning to behave like a wild horse. Anika was holding onto the board at the head of the bed.

'Maritz was talking to the Deputy Transport Minister on the phone,' Anika said slowly, 'about his business being good for Alexandria. Maybe the Minister of Transport and the Harbourmaster didn't think it was. But that's no reason to kill them.'

Zaphira sat down again. 'People like Maritz don't understand any language but power.' She swallowed and put her hand on her stomach. Her face was pale in the dull light and she seemed to be sweating. Her long hair was wilder than ever.

Anika went on, 'But Ahmed works at the new airport. How could he get involved with people like that? How could Maritz persuade him to …? No! I'll never believe—'

Zaphira suddenly jumped up and ran into the bathroom.

Anika could hear Zaphira being sick into the toilet. 'Are you all right?' she called softly, but Zaphira didn't answer. Anika stood up to go into the bathroom to help, holding onto the wall-rail.

Zaphira waved her back. 'I'm OK,' she said, and then groaned again as her stomach disagreed.

Chapter 10 *Mirror*

Anika heard a man walking along the corridor, falling against the walls and swearing in Arabic. From his voice, she knew it was the man with the moustache. The glass door opened and banged against the wall before it closed again.

Someone quieter went along the corridor. Anika hoped Zaphira could not be heard above the noises of the yacht and the rising wind.

There was a scratching noise on the door and it swung open and shut. Musaid had two bottles of water in his hand. Anika did not dare let go of the rail.

'Everything OK?' asked Musaid, holding on to the door handle. He threw the bottles onto the bed.

'Fine,' said Anika. 'Thanks for those.'

'Where's your friend?'

'In the bathroom.'

There was a pause. They heard Zaphira groan.

'Who were those two people?' Anika asked him. 'We could see from the window …'

Musaid looked out at the dark sky and huge waves with a worried frown. 'Well, the big man with the moustache is called Karimi. I don't know who the other one is. He was unconscious when we carried him on board.'

Zaphira groaned again.

Musaid looked towards the bathroom. 'Is she all right?'

'Seasick, I suppose,' said Anika. 'She was fine until the storm started. Tell me about Karimi.'

Zaphira came out of the bathroom, holding a towel to her mouth. Musaid smiled at her.

'Who is Karimi?' asked Zaphira through her towel.

'He's the man with the moustache you saw from the window. He works for Mr Maritz. I've only seen him a couple of times,' said Musaid.

The yacht suddenly seemed to jump and they all had to grab the wall-rail.

'I'd better get back,' said Musaid. He smiled at Zaphira. 'Anything else you need?'

'We're fine,' said Zaphira.

'Thanks,' said Anika.

Musaid went out and locked the door behind him.

Suddenly, the yacht crashed down from the top of a wave. The piece of rail that Zaphira was holding onto came off the wall. She was thrown across the room at the large mirror. The rail in her hand smashed the glass.

That crash was louder than the sounds of the storm. Bits of mirror fell to the floor, like a waterfall of shining knives. Anika had let go of the rail for a moment and fallen so that she was sitting on the floor.

Zaphira was still on her feet. She dropped the broken piece of rail and looked at her hands. No cuts! But another roll of the yacht threw her onto the bed. She was trying to get up when the door handle rattled loudly.

'What's going on?' they heard in English in the corridor. 'Why is this door locked? Where are you, Musaid?' It was Maritz.

Then they heard Musaid's voice, coming nearer. Zaphira was sitting on the bed and Anika was on the floor near the pile of mirror pieces. They stared at the door.

'Not in that cabin, Mr Maritz sir,' said Musaid loudly in English. 'I think the noise came from across the corridor.'

Zaphira grabbed her bag and Anika's. She had the key in her other hand. 'Come on!' she whispered loudly, 'while they're in another cabin. Quick!'

Anika pulled herself up on the wall-rail and reached the door just as Zaphira opened it. Across the corridor, one door was swinging wildly open and shut, and the other was closed.

Zaphira stepped quickly across to the closed door and pushed it open. Anika followed her.

As they shut and locked the door behind them, they heard Maritz shout at Musaid, 'Look at that door! It's wide open. It was locked before! What are you up to, Musaid?'

'It must have got stuck, sir. That can happen with the damp on a yacht.'

'I know that!' shouted Maritz. Then his voice was further away. 'Look at this mirror! What the hell happened here?'

The girls heard Musaid say something. A few moments later, they heard someone lock the door of their old cabin and go through the glass door.

'Wow!' said Zaphira. 'That was close!'

'You're bleeding!' said Anika suddenly. 'Your forehead.'

Zaphira went into the bathroom. She tried to wash her face with one hand while holding on with the other. Anika held onto the wall-rail with her right hand. She felt as if her good arm was being pulled off by the motion of the yacht.

'It's just a little cut,' whispered Zaphira. 'It doesn't hurt.'

The cabin was exactly like the one they had left except that the armchairs were attached to the floor, facing the window. Zaphira put their bags in a cupboard. They fell into the chairs and watched as the line of the sky outside rose up and down.

Anika said, 'Should we try and communicate with Ahmed?'

'Not now,' said Zaphira. She shut her eyes, her hands on her stomach.

A few seconds later, she said, 'If they do find us, we should pretend we don't understand them.' She opened her eyes and looked hard at Anika. 'That way, they'll think we're harmless and we'll have a better chance of getting away.'

'Act stupid, you mean?' Anika asked.

'Not suspiciously stupid,' replied Zaphira. 'Just that we don't understand English. Maritz seems very dangerous. He'll kill us if he suspects we could damage him.'

'Right,' said Anika. 'Me no spik Anglish.'

Zaphira smiled and groaned. 'Too right, you don't,' she said in Arabic, holding her stomach.

* * *

It was fully dark when Anika woke, and the sea was smooth. Zaphira was shaking her arm. Anika could hear someone trying to unlock the cabin door.

Zaphira was saying urgently, 'Is your phone hidden?'

'Yes,' Anika said as she woke up. 'What about yours?'

Zaphira stood up as someone kicked the door. 'I don't think we're going to be able to hide this time. No English!' she added. 'Don't forget!'

Anika stood up and faced the door. She felt strangely calm.

The door suddenly gave way with a crash. Karimi, the man with the moustache, fell into the cabin, followed by Musaid.

'Come here!' shouted Karimi in Arabic at Anika. 'Musaid, get the other one!' His voice was like the bark of a large dog. He grabbed both of Anika's hands. 'Come with me!' he said, and pulled her to the door.

The sudden pain made Anika scream.

Chapter 11 *Maritz*

The pain was terrible, but screaming made it bearable. So Anika screamed again as she was pulled along the corridor towards the glass door.

Musaid and Zaphira were behind her. Musaid shouted in Arabic, 'She has a wound, Mr Karimi. She bleeds from her shoulder.'

Karimi stopped for a moment to open the glass door. Then he pulled Anika into a large white room with windows on three sides. There were cream-coloured sofas against the walls, a dark blue carpet, and white coffee tables here and there. A large television hung on the wall by the door. At the other end of this long cabin, another door opened onto the deck at the front of the yacht. It was dark outside.

But that door was closed, and standing in front of it was Maritz, his arms across his chest. He was dressed in loose white trousers and a pale blue T-shirt.

Anika stopped screaming, and held her burning shoulder with her right hand. Zaphira moved to stand in front of her, as if to protect her.

'Well now,' said Maritz in English, his voice sweet and musical. 'What have you found, Karimi, my man?'

Anika couldn't help staring at Maritz. Zaphira was right: he looked like a film star. His thick blond hair fell across his forehead. He was smiling, and his bright blue eyes and white teeth shone in his suntanned face. His T-shirt was stretched tight over his muscular chest.

Maritz looked at the girls as if he were considering a delicious meal. 'What's your name, flame-of-my-heart?' he said to Zaphira, licking his lips.

Zaphira made an I-don't-understand face.

'And how about you, delight-of-my-eyes?' he said to Anika.

Anika shook her head. She felt sick with pain and fear.

Maritz stopped smiling. 'Karimi, find out who they are,' he ordered.

'What are your names?' Karimi barked in Arabic. 'How did you get on the boat?'

Zaphira shook her head slightly at Anika, who was trying to think in a fog of pain.

'Come on!' said Karimi. 'Tell me your name!' He grabbed Anika's left arm and tried to pull it up behind her back.

She screamed again. Karimi kept hold of her.

Zaphira took a step towards them, but Musaid said in English, 'They must be the missing girls from the bombing.'

Anika was gasping with the pain, but she guessed Zaphira was planning an attack. She shouted in Arabic, 'Don't!'

But she was too late. Zaphira turned on one foot and kicked Karimi on the back of his head. He fell to the floor, with Anika underneath him. She cried out, and he swore. Anika felt him pull a gun out of his pocket as he tried to stand up, and caught hold of his sleeve to pull him down again.

Maritz called out, 'Grab the tall one, Musaid!'

Karimi pulled Anika's fingers off his sleeve. Anika grabbed his leg as a shot rang out.

Everyone froze.

Maritz had jumped onto one of the seats. The bullet seemed to have missed everyone. Zaphira was standing in front of Maritz, and Musaid was holding her arms to her sides. Karimi pointed his gun at her. 'Don't move!' he said in Arabic through his teeth, his eyes wild with anger.

'Well now, thank you, Karimi, wolf-of-the-streets,' said Maritz as he jumped smoothly down from the seat. 'What presence of mind you have. And what exciting guests we have.' He laughed as he looked into Zaphira's face. 'Aren't you, flame-of-my-heart?'

Zaphira looked directly at him with a sad smile, and shook her head. Then she said to Musaid. 'Let me go now. I need to help her,' and she nodded towards Anika. Musaid let go of her arms. She ignored Karimi and his gun, and went to help Anika get up and sit on one of the pale leather seats.

'That girl's pouring blood everywhere,' complained Maritz. 'Did you shoot her?'

'No,' said Karimi. 'She was already wounded.'

'OK,' said Maritz, his voice icy now. 'Musaid, clean up this mess and then see to the wound. And Karimi, lock them up. When we get to Faliron, arrange to keep them safe. If she *is* that missing girl, she could make us rich.' This made him smile again. 'Rich, richer, richest,' he said with a laugh.

Then he went up to Zaphira, put his hand under her chin and said, 'We might even have some fun, mightn't we?'

Zaphira grabbed Maritz's hand in both hers and bit his thumb. Maritz jumped back. 'You made me bleed!' he shouted in surprise. 'Oh, I'm going to love playing with *you*!'

At that moment Anika cried, 'Behind you, Zaphira!'

And Karimi punched Zaphira low down in her back.

Zaphira cried out with pain, and turned angrily to face him. He waved his gun at her and said, 'This way. I'll shoot your toes off, one by one, if you don't behave.'

Karimi pushed them along the corridor and into the room with the broken mirror. He went out and locked the door.

Anika fell face down on the bed. Zaphira asked quietly, 'Are you OK?'

'I think so,' Anika replied. She was shaking and trying not to be sick.

Musaid came in. He washed and dressed Anika's wound. She was sweating, although she felt cold.

When he had finished, he left, taking away a large pile of bloody bandages and locking the door. He didn't speak.

Anika turned on her side. She tried to think about something other than the pain. 'How's your back?' she asked. It was a relief not to have to whisper.

'I'll get over it,' said Zaphira. 'You get some sleep. Oh, and thanks for what you did in there.'

'It's amazing no one died.' Anika could hardly speak.

'Well, I promise not to kill anyone till you wake up.'

Anika sighed. 'You really are–'

Zaphira shook her head. 'No, Anika. I'm not crazy. Maritz is crazy. Scary crazy – mad. You just have to listen to him to know that. I'm just … trying to help.'

Every part of Anika's body seemed to hurt. 'Well, help then,' she said. 'Help us stay alive, until we can get out of this.' And she shut her eyes.

Chapter 12 *Inspection*

Anika must have slept, because she opened her eyes to bright daylight. The engine was silent.

Karimi was standing over her. She couldn't see Zaphira.

'Get up! Go in the bathroom,' he said roughly in Arabic.

Anika stood up slowly. She was dizzy and the fire in her shoulder still burned. Zaphira was in the bathroom, sitting on the side of the bath. Her hands and feet were tied together. The shower curtain behind her was closed. Anika turned to Karimi in confusion.

'Why have you tied her up?' she asked.

Karimi said, 'She's dangerous. You both stay in here and keep quiet. I'll be in the bedroom.' He took his gun out of his pocket. 'No noise!'

He shut the door and they heard him moving around, picking up bits of the broken mirror.

Zaphira said, 'We must have arrived in Faliron. I think he's expecting someone from the harbour authorities to check their passports, and they don't want us to be found.'

'But the man from the authorities could be our only chance to get a message out,' said Anika urgently.

'I think trying to speak to him might start a shooting match. Let's stay alive, as you said. We'll be on land soon.'

Anika sighed and sat on the closed toilet seat. 'If you hadn't been so aggressive to Maritz and Karimi, they wouldn't have tied you up.'

'No,' said Zaphira with a smile. 'They're afraid of me now.'

'Maybe I can untie you.'

'I doubt you could manage with only one good hand. And we don't know how long we've got before Karimi opens the door. Leave it for now. If the harbour authorities man does find us, and I'm still tied up, he'll see we're prisoners.'

'Like Ahmed,' said Anika.

'They'll be hiding him too, I expect,' said Zaphira. 'I got caught before I had a chance to look for him.'

There were voices in the corridor and the girls heard their cabin door open. 'That mirror's broken,' said a man in English. 'Broken mirror means bad luck.'

'Good morning, Mr Inspector,' said Karimi pleasantly. 'Yes, it broke in the storm.'

'Hmm. According to my list, you are Sayid El-Karimi?'

'That's right.' The girls heard some pages being turned and guessed it was Karimi's passport.

'I've seen Musaid Diab, Malcolm Maritz, and the captain and two crew. There's no one else on the boat?'

'That's right,' said Karimi again.

'OK,' said the inspector. 'The door to the cabin opposite is broken, too.'

'Yes,' said Karimi. 'It got stuck. I had to move in there when the mirror broke.'

'I'll just take a look.' The inspector's voice moved away.

'Fine,' said Karimi, following him.

A moment later, the door of the bathroom opened. It was Musaid. He whispered in Arabic, 'Karimi has told me to guard you.' Then he said more loudly, 'I'm just outside and I've got a gun.'

'OK. We'll stay here and be quiet,' said Anika, standing up.

Musaid shut the bathroom door.

'Look in the bath,' Zaphira whispered.

Anika lifted the shower curtain quietly and saw their bags.

'Change into your trainers now,' whispered Zaphira. 'If we have to run, the shoes you're wearing will make a noise.'

Anika managed to change her street shoes for her trainers. She took her cell phone out of the bottom of the trainer and hid it again in one of her street shoes. Then she put the street shoes into her sports bag. 'How did you get our bags from the other cabin?' she asked Zaphira.

Zaphira said, 'I got them while you were asleep. No one noticed.' She smiled. 'I still had the cabin key in my pocket. Look, when we leave, can you manage both bags?'

'I'll have to, won't I?' said Anika, shaking her head in disbelief. 'Did they catch you when you got the bags? Is that why they tied you up?'

'No,' Zaphira said. 'That was a few minutes later. Karimi tied me up because I almost got his gun off him.'

'Zaphira!' Anika cried. 'Please stop taking mad risks!'

'He searched me and found my knife.'

'That's no reason to–'

'It was my brother's penknife. It's the only thing of his I still have – had.' Zaphira's eyes dared Anika to argue with her.

Anika bit her lip and her eyes filled with tears. 'I'm so sorry,' she said. She looked down at the ropes round Zaphira's ankles. 'How are you going to walk now?' she said.

Zaphira looked down, too. 'I'll jump!' she said.

Anika smiled through her tears. 'You never give up, do you?' she said.

Just then, Musaid pulled the bathroom door open again.

'Time to move!' he said. 'You have transport!'

'How can I move?' asked Zaphira, pointing at her feet.

Karimi appeared behind Musaid.

'What are those?' he demanded, waving his gun at the bags in the bath.

'Just our basketball stuff,' said Anika. 'No money, nothing valuable, nothing dangerous.'

'Get them!' he said to Musaid.

When the bags were on the floor of the cabin, Karimi ordered Musaid to search them.

Anika didn't dare watch in case she showed her fear. Musaid didn't find the cell phone in her shoe, but he found Zaphira's.

'It's dead,' said Zaphira. 'Useless.'

'Hmm,' said Karimi. He leant towards Zaphira with an ugly smile, her knife open in his hand.

Zaphira stood up very tall and stared at him.

Then he bent down and used the knife to cut the ropes round her ankles. He closed the knife, dropped it into his pocket, and waved his gun at the girls.

'Go on,' he said. 'Into the corridor and down the stairs.'

Musaid went first, carrying their bags. The girls followed him. Karimi came behind them, his gun pointing steadily at Zaphira's head.

Chapter 13   *Kidnap*

At the bottom of the stairs, Karimi pushed Anika and Zaphira through a door into bright sunlight. They could hear harbour sounds and it was already very hot. A long black car was parked beside a large white van. 'Walk down slowly and get into the car,' he said in Arabic. 'Mr Maritz is waiting for you. Don't try running away!'

The girls could see a grey wall with a tall fence above it in front of them, but they couldn't see past the white van.

The back door of the car was open and Karimi pushed the girls in. Maritz sat alone on the wide back seat. He ordered Anika and Karimi to sit on the two small seats in front of him with their backs to the driver. There was no sign of Ahmed.

'And you, wild woman,' he said to Zaphira, 'you sit on the floor. So friendly, just like the family at home.'

'Maybe see you later,' said Musaid, closing the car door.

The car moved off. It was cool inside and the windows were dark, but Anika could see enough to know they were in busy traffic. They drove along a wide street by the sea, towards the morning sun. There were blocks of flats side by side on the left. On the right was a tramline, and beyond that, the bright sea. It reminded Anika of the Corniche in Alexandria, but the buildings here were taller and newer. Motorbikes and cars passed them on both sides.

Maritz leaned forward and took hold of some of Zaphira's cloud of brown hair. 'We're going to have a lot of fun after

I've dealt with my business today,' he said in his smoothest voice. Zaphira looked at him coldly, daring him to hurt her.

Karimi said in English, 'I've taken on two women guards. Don't want anyone spoiling the girls for you.'

Maritz laughed. He let go of Zaphira's hair and said to Karimi. 'And how is our sweet bomber-boy today?'

Anika looked at Zaphira, but she was looking at the floor of the car. 'Of course,' thought Anika. 'I'm not supposed to understand any of this. I wish I didn't.' She looked out of the window at the trees and a tram that they were passing.

'He's fine,' Karimi said. 'He'll be safe and sound on the yacht with Musaid until we get him back to Alexandria.'

Maritz's cell phone rang. 'He'd better be,' he said as he took the phone out of his pocket and looked at the screen.

'Ah, Mr Bryant!' he said into the phone with friendly warmth. 'What can I do for you? … You can't make it to the yacht? … Ah. This afternoon. I see. … Marathon? … Well now.' Maritz's voice went from warm to cool. 'I'll have to re-arrange things with my accountant and my lawyer.'

Anika studied the shine of the sea flashing between the trees by the road. They passed a statue of a man on a horse.

Maritz went on, 'I'll see what they can manage and get back to you. … Well, that's very good of you. I look forward to meeting your wife and daughters. It sounds like the perfect beach holiday. … I'll be in touch within the hour. … Goodbye, Mr Bryant.'

Maritz put his phone away. No one spoke.

Zaphira lay down on the floor and closed her eyes.

Maritz spoke over her to Karimi. 'I'll need you with me later,' he said.

Anika looked from Karimi to Maritz with a carefully stupid expression on her face.

Maritz's eyes were ice-blue. 'I'm not sure I like leaving bomber-boy on the yacht,' he said. 'If I'd had my way, he'd be safely at the bottom of the sea by now. Make sure he's worth the trouble he's causing, Karimi.'

'Oh, he will be.' Karimi smiled. Under his moustache, his teeth were surprisingly white. 'Ahmed will do anything I want now. If he doesn't, his mother will die a slow and painful death, and he'll be hanged for the bombing.'

Anika looked out of the window again to hide the horror in her eyes. She counted five motorbikes in the traffic beside the car. She thought, 'Was that why Ahmed planted the bomb, to save his mother? Have they kidnapped her, too?'

Karimi went on, 'Ahmed is your guarantee of help with your new business at the airport, Mr Maritz.'

'If I ever get it started,' said Maritz impatiently. He looked down at Zaphira, who was pretending to be asleep on the floor. He pushed her with his foot. 'Wake up, wild woman! We're nearly there.'

As Zaphira stirred, the car turned off the main road into a narrow street with parked cars and trees on either side. They passed a school and Anika could hear children playing. The car turned into a walled yard through a gate which closed behind it.

Two women pulled the car doors open, reached in, and grabbed the girls and their bags. They led Anika and Zaphira roughly into the house.

The girls were pushed down some steps, through a heavy door and into a room with one light bulb hanging from the ceiling. Everything was grey. There were no windows.

Against the walls there were two narrow beds. In the wall opposite the door was an empty doorway. A toilet and a sink showed white in the tiny room beyond.

The women didn't speak. They pushed the girls onto the beds, dropped their bags, and locked the door as they left.

Anika looked around. 'At least the room's not moving like the yacht,' she said.

Zaphira stood up and came over. She leant down and whispered in Arabic, 'There will be microphones. They may not understand Arabic, but we know they speak English.'

Anika looked into Zaphira's tiger-brown eyes and nodded.

They began a loud conversation about how hopeless and frightened they felt, while Anika worked on untying the ropes around Zaphira's wrists. It was hard because Anika felt so ill and the knots were tied so tight.

When at last the ropes fell away, Zaphira went to Anika's sports bag and took out the bandages she'd put there. She unrolled them and hung them over the end of her bed.

Anika was puzzled. 'What are those for?' she whispered.

Zaphira whispered in Anika's ear, 'If someone comes, we'll attack them and tie them up. OK?'

'Couldn't we just offer them money to free us?'

'But we haven't got any money,' said Zaphira.

Anika felt too ill to argue. 'OK,' she sighed.

Just then, the door was unlocked, and the two women came in with food. The shorter woman carried a tray. The taller woman went towards the bathroom.

'Ready?' breathed Zaphira in Arabic as the smaller woman bent down to put the tray on the floor.

Anika took a deep breath and nodded.

Chapter 14   *Over the gate*

Zaphira said, 'Now!' and jumped at the taller woman. She grabbed her shoulders, turned her around, and drove her own forehead into the woman's nose. She fell towards Zaphira, who brought her knee up hard into the woman's stomach.

Meanwhile, Anika had pushed the second woman over. She fell, hitting her head on the side of the bed, and lay still. Anika thought shakily, 'What have I done?'

The taller woman was on her knees, coughing. Zaphira kicked the keys out of her hand. Then she tied the woman's hands behind her back with a bandage. The woman took a breath to shout. Zaphira hit her in the throat and tied another bandage across her mouth.

The smaller woman began to move, but Anika quickly sat on her back. Zaphira tied bandages around the woman's hands and mouth. The women were making a lot of noise through the bandages in their mouths. Zaphira searched them and found a phone, but no weapons.

Anika had their sports bags in her good hand. Zaphira nodded at her and they went through the door fast. Zaphira locked it behind them and ran silently up the steps.

At the top, Zaphira put her finger to her lips. She took the bags from Anika as they stood still and listened.

They could hear Karimi's voice not far away, talking on a phone. Behind them, the women were getting noisier.

The girls were at one end of a corridor. At the other end, sunlight shone through the window in a black door.

Zaphira stepped into the corridor and signed to Anika to follow. They walked silently in their trainers towards the black door.

Karimi had his back to them as they passed the open doorway of the room he was in. There was no sign of Maritz. The handle of the black door turned easily, and suddenly they were outside in the heat and blinding sunlight.

This was not the way they had come into the house. There was a yard with pink and orange flowering plants growing up high walls. To their right there was a gate made of iron bent into complicated patterns. It looked easy to climb.

They heard noises from the house and ran to the gate.

Zaphira helped Anika up and over. She threw the bags to Anika and quickly climbed over herself.

They were in a steep, narrow street leading uphill to their right. There were small trees up there, and bushes with pink flowers growing in square holes in the pavement. A few cars were parked by the roadside, but there was no good place to hide.

The girls ran up the hill. They heard a shout and ran faster. They turned right into another street and hid behind a car. Anika could hardly stand, she was so breathless and dizzy.

They could hear voices speaking in English. 'Down that way,' one said.

The girls couldn't hear the next words clearly.

Anika thought she was going to be sick. Zaphira looked over the top of the car as a man walked round the corner.

She whispered, 'Stay down and be quiet!'

They heard the man walking towards the car. They moved round it silently to stay hidden from him.

The man stood on the other side of the car and said in English, 'I won't hurt you. I'm a policeman.' He held up his badge. 'Who are you, and why are you running away?'

*   *   *

Within minutes, the girls found themselves in the back of a small, unmarked police car. The man who had found them was in the front, beside the driver. He turned to them. He had a tired face and needed a shave. His hair was short and going grey. He was tall and strong, but his eyes were a gentle green. He said in English, 'So now you know that I am Nikos Drakopoulos and I work for Interpol. And you say you are Anika Hakim and Zaphira Bakkal, but can you prove it?'

The car was on a main road now, going fast. Anika sighed and shook her head. She was finding it hard to concentrate, she felt so shaky and sick. 'We have nothing to identify us,' she said in English.

'Wait,' said Zaphira in Arabic. 'Your notebook. In your bag. Shall I show him?'

Anika nodded. Zaphira found the notebook and gave it to Nikos. She said in English, 'You see. Her name?'

Nikos looked at Anika's name written neatly in Arabic and English on the cover. He turned a few pages. 'You draw well,' he said. Then he turned round and took out his cell phone. He spoke into it in Greek. They heard their names.

Zaphira and Anika looked at each other. Then Anika felt everything go grey and her head fell forward as she fainted.

Chapter 15 *Netta*

Anika's shoulder was hurting a lot. She was lying on her face on a bed. She was in hospital, and someone was making her pain worse. 'Ayayai!' she groaned. 'Please stop!' she said in English.

'Finished,' said a woman's voice with a Greek accent. 'You can sit up now.'

Anika was very dizzy, but managed to sit.

A nurse was standing by the bed, holding a glass of water. 'Here,' she said. 'Take these pills. They're painkillers and antibiotics.'

Anika swallowed the pills. She was very thirsty, and drank the whole glass of water.

The nurse gave Anika a small package and said, 'Take two of these every six hours. We have sewn up your wound. You'll be OK now.'

Then Anika saw Zaphira standing further away.

In Arabic, Zaphira said, 'They say we have to go to the police headquarters nearby. There we can phone home. And do you want anything to eat?'

'Oh thank God!' Anika said. 'Phone first, then eat.'

* * *

A policeman in uniform led them out of the hospital. They crossed a wide road in the hot sun. Anika held on to Zaphira's arm. They walked into the shade of a large building with a blue notice outside which said something in Greek, and 'Hellenic Police Headquarters' in English. They were led inside and went up in a lift. Then they were taken to a cool room with a large window which looked over the city. Buildings stretched all the way to the sea, which was now a long way away. Further away, on the skyline, there were islands. Between the islands and the city, the bright sea was dotted with ships.

A middle-aged woman was waiting for them by a table with a white telephone on it and four chairs around it.

'My name is Netta,' she said in English. 'I work for Interpol. Do you understand?'

Anika and Zaphira nodded.

Netta had short dark hair and a long nose. She went on, 'You are now in the European Union, but you have no identity papers. You will be sent back to Egypt at the first opportunity.'

Zaphira said, 'That's fine. We didn't *want* to come here.'

'I know that,' said Netta. 'But we have to follow the rules. If you wish, we will get in touch with your embassy immediately. But Interpol prefers to avoid the publicity that that would probably bring. We are examining your bags and checking your story. If you want to call your families, you can do that from here. You are being watched, of course.' Netta pointed to a CCTV camera high up on the wall.

'Where are we exactly?' asked Anika.

'The Interpol offices of the Greek police in Athens.'

'You call first,' said Zaphira to Anika, and she walked over to the window and looked out. Netta left the room.

Anika sat at the table and picked up the telephone. Her hand shook. Her grandmother answered and wouldn't believe at first that it was Anika. When at last she did, she got Anika's brother Gamal to come to the phone.

'Is that really you?' he asked. He was almost crying.

'Yes, it's me,' Anika said. 'I'm OK. The Greek police are going to send us home very soon.' She was half laughing, half crying herself.

Gamal said, 'I thought I had killed you – you and your friend – by being late.'

'No!' Anika almost shouted. 'No! It wasn't your fault. We're safe now. We'll tell you the whole story when we get back. I want Zaphira to use the phone now.'

'I'll come and get you,' said her brother.

Anika laughed. 'Don't be crazy! We'll be home tomorrow.'

'See you soon,' he said. 'Thank God you're safe.'

'Give my love to everyone. See you soon,' said Anika, and hung up.

Zaphira came over from the window. 'Finished?' she asked with a strange, hard look in her eyes.

'Of course,' said Anika. 'Do you want to sit here …'

'No, I'm fine,' said Zaphira. 'Just give me the phone.'

She stayed standing and dialled. After a moment, she said, 'Hi, Mum,' and there was a long pause. 'It's not my fault, Mum. Ahmed dragged us away. We didn't know …' There was another pause. Zaphira sat on the edge of the table.

Anika began to wish she was in another room.

Zaphira held the phone away from her ear. She looked angry and hurt at the same time.

Netta came in with Anika's notebook. She spoke quietly to Anika in English. 'They are trying to mend your cell phone. I wanted to ask you who the pictures in your notebook are.'

Zaphira was still holding the phone at arm's length.

'OK,' said Anika as Netta gave her a pencil. Anika wrote the names of the people she had drawn in English. There were drawings of her grandmother, her father, Gamal, her other two brothers, friends from school and basketball.

Zaphira put the phone to her ear again. 'We're in Athens,' she said. 'In Greece. I'll let you know when we'll be back.' Then she said the same thing again, but louder, and hung up.

Anika came to the page in her notebook with Ahmed's face. She felt herself going red, but wrote his name, Ahmed Bakkal, in the corner.

Netta was surprised. She said, 'You know Ahmed Bakkal?'

Anika looked up at Zaphira with frightened eyes. Then she turned to Netta. 'Yes,' she said. 'He comes sometimes and watches us training for basketball.'

'Why are you asking?' Zaphira asked Netta in English.

'He has the same surname as you, and I heard an officer mention him a few minutes ago,' said Netta. She looked at Zaphira. 'Is he a relative?'

'Cousin,' said Zaphira.

Anika looked at Zaphira with a confused frown. How could Interpol know Ahmed's name?

Chapter 16   *Rees Meyers*

Two hours later, the girls still didn't know how Interpol knew Ahmed's name. They had been interviewed again by another officer and had answered a lot of questions. Anika had begun to feel a little better. The pills the nurse had given her seemed to be working.

At 12.45 p.m. Nikos came in with a tray of sandwiches and soft drinks.

'I've brought your statements for you to sign,' he said. 'Please read them through carefully to check that we wrote everything down correctly.'

Zaphira said, 'But first, can you tell us why Interpol is interested in Ahmed Bakkal?'

Nikos sat down. 'It seems,' he said, 'that a man with that name gave himself up to the Faliron police earlier today.'

Anika was delighted. 'So Ahmed escaped from the yacht!'

'Where is he now?' asked Zaphira.

'In the hospital across the road,' said Nikos. 'I'm afraid you can't see him. He is in the operating theatre. He has broken bones in his chest and deep cuts to his head.'

Anika said, 'And can you also tell us how you knew we were in Maritz's house?'

Nikos smiled. 'I didn't,' he said. 'Interpol has a "Blue Notice" out for Maritz. This means we're actively trying to get evidence against him. But he doesn't usually set foot in Europe. So when Customs told us that he arrived at Faliron this morning on his yacht, I went to take a look. I couldn't see who got into his car because there was a white van in the way, so I followed the car when it left. I was nearby, watching Maritz's house, when you climbed over the gate. As soon as I saw you, I guessed you might be the missing girls,' said Nikos, 'because Maritz's yacht had come from Alexandria. Now,' he stood up. 'I want you to sign these statements so we can arrange for you to go home. But there's something else I have to ask you first.'

'Go ahead,' said Zaphira.

'You both say in your statements that you think Karimi forced Ahmed to plant the bomb by kidnapping his mother on Maritz's orders. I am hoping that Ahmed's evidence will support yours. But you also mention that Maritz phoned a Mr Bryant this morning to arrange a meeting.'

'Yes,' said Anika and Zaphira together.

'Well, we have found a Mr Bryant who agrees that he is in the middle of a deal to sell his small airline to a man from South Africa. But that man is called Rees Meyers, not Malcolm Maritz.' There was a hard edge to Nikos' voice.

Zaphira looked at Nikos coldly. 'You don't believe us.'

'Much of what you say has not been proved yet,' said Nikos.

Anika shook her head in confusion. 'But we heard Maritz make the appointment with Bryant,' she said.

Nikos sighed. 'What did he say exactly?'

Anika looked at Zaphira, who said, 'Mr Bryant wanted to change the time and place of the meeting. Maritz didn't like that much.'

Anika nodded. 'And then he said something about a marathon,' she said.

'A marathon? You mean a race?' asked Nikos in confusion.

'I … I'm not sure I understood,' said Anika, feeling stupid. 'I mean, I'm interested in marathon races. I've started training for them. Aren't they supposed to be in memory of a soldier who ran to Athens to tell the Athenians they'd won a battle or something?'

Nikos frowned. 'That's right. In 490 BC. The Greeks had just beaten the Persians at Marathon.'

Anika said, 'I don't know why Maritz would talk about that, but he certainly said the word marathon.'

'Perhaps he meant the place, not the race,' said Nikos.

'Is there a beach?' asked Zaphira suddenly.

'Yes,' said Nikos, 'there is. Why?'

'Maritz said something about Mr Bryant and his family having the perfect beach holiday,' said Zaphira.

'You mean Mr Bryant is staying there?' Nikos stood up. 'He didn't tell me that when I spoke to him.'

'That's what I understood,' said Zaphira.

'With his family?'

'Yes. Maritz mentioned Mr Bryant's wife and daughters,' said Anika.

'Did they agree a time for this meeting?' Nikos had his phone in his hand.

'No,' said Anika. 'Maritz said he would be in touch with Mr Bryant again within the hour.'

'I'll be back in five minutes,' said Nikos, and went out.

Chapter 17 *Red notice*

The girls went over to the window.

Anika said, 'What do you think will happen to Ahmed?'

'They'll send him home when he's well enough, I suppose,' said Zaphira looking down at the city, misty in the heat.

Nikos came back.

'What did Mr Bryant say?' asked Zaphira.

'Netta's working on it,' said Nikos.

Anika said, 'Can you tell us what will happen to Ahmed?'

'He's in Greece without papers and he has admitted he planted the Qaitbay bomb.'

Anika bit her lip to stop herself crying.

Nikos went on, 'So when he is able to make and sign a statement, we'll hand him over to the Egyptian police.' Nikos put the girls' statements on the table again.

Zaphira looked at Nikos. 'Ahmed will be sentenced to death, you know,' she said.

'He's admitted his guilt,' said Nikos simply.

'NO!' shouted Zaphira suddenly. 'No! He should *not* die when he was trying to save his mother's life!'

Nikos looked surprised. 'But what can I do about that?'

'You can make sure you get Maritz, and that he makes a confession.' Zaphira's fierce eyes didn't leave his face. 'You can make sure the truth is told! That's your job, isn't it?'

Nikos looked at her calmly. 'And that's what I'm doing,' he said. 'We are checking that statements and evidence agree. When we are sure of that, we will arrest Maritz.'

'And when will that be?' asked Zaphira.

'I don't know exactly,' said Nikos. 'Maybe in the next few days. We have your statements now. And we should have Ahmed's by tomorrow.'

'And by then Maritz will have left,' said Zaphira. 'You don't understand. He's totally mad. He could do anything, go anywhere, change his identity. You must arrest him now!'

Nikos looked angry. 'And how do you suggest we do that?' he said. 'He's in this country with the correct papers. At the moment, your evidence wouldn't stand up in court.'

Zaphira was almost as tall as Nikos. She looked him in the eye and asked, 'If Maritz admitted that he ordered the bomb, would Ahmed still be sentenced to death?'

Nikos was surprised. 'No,' he said, 'I don't think so. I don't know anything about Egyptian law, but in Europe he would go to prison for a shorter time.'

'So,' said Zaphira, 'if you arrest Maritz today, you may save Ahmed's life, *and* stop Maritz killing someone else. And–'

The door opened and Netta came in.

'I need to speak to Nikos for a minute,' she said.

Netta and Nikos spoke together in Greek.

Anika watched them and realised that Netta must be Nikos' boss. He didn't like what Netta was saying, but he seemed to agree to it after an argument.

At last, Netta turned to the girls.

'I have been in touch with our head office in Lyon,' she said. 'We think, but cannot yet prove, that Rees Meyers and Malcolm Maritz are the same man. It seems that Mr Wahab stopped Maritz from using part of Alexandria harbour for his ships. Mr Wahab believed that Maritz wanted to use it as a route for smuggling weapons. Interpol has changed the Blue Notice to a Red Notice. We are to arrest Maritz and Karimi while they are in Greece.'

'Fantastic!' said Zaphira, her eyes shining.

Nikos said something to Netta in Greek.

'Of course,' she answered in English and turned to the girls. 'We have to hurry. Mr Bryant has agreed to allow someone to take his place at the meeting – a false Mr Bryant will meet "Mr Meyers".'

'That false Mr Bryant will be me,' said Nikos.

'And I will be Mrs Bryant,' said Netta. 'We will meet this "Mr Meyers" and, if it's Maritz, we'll arrest him.'

'How will you know it's him?' asked Zaphira.

'We have a photo,' said Nikos.

'But he may look different,' said Zaphira.

Netta looked at Zaphira. 'What are you saying?'

Zaphira put her hands on the table and leant towards Netta. She said, 'I can positively identify him as Maritz. I want to be there when you meet him.'

Nikos looked shocked.

Anika gasped and said, 'But he would recognise you, Zaphira! He won't even speak to Mr Bryant if he sees you.'

'I don't need to be visible,' said Zaphira.

Netta turned to Nikos and they spoke urgently in Greek.

Anika said in Arabic, 'Please, Zaphira. Don't do this. It could be very dangerous. If Karimi is there as well …'

'Don't you see?' said Zaphira. 'The police have to get Maritz now. And I have to get Ahmed the shortest possible sentence. If my brother were alive, he would do this.'

'But you're not your brother,' said Anika.

'No,' said Zaphira sadly. 'I am much more intelligent.'

'It's not intelligent to get yourself killed! Anything could happen at that meeting.'

Netta turned to the girls and said in English, 'We agree you can come, Zaphira. It would be very helpful to have proof that Mr Meyers and Mr Maritz are the same person.'

'But you must not be recognised or hurt,' said Nikos.

'So we must change your appearance,' said Netta.

'And you must keep your distance from Maritz and his men,' said Nikos.

'Of course,' said Zaphira straight away.

'And, as Mr Bryant has two daughters,' said Netta, looking at Anika, 'we hope you will agree to come, too.'

'Me?' cried Anika. 'What can I do? He would know me immediately!' She touched her bandaged shoulder.

'You can also change your appearance, and stay upstairs on the balcony of the house,' said Nikos. 'This is Mr Bryant's beach house near Marathon, where the meeting will take place.' He showed them a picture on his cell phone of a large, two-storey house with a swimming pool in front of it. There were wide balconies at the front and at the back on the first floor.

'It will add to the family atmosphere and make Maritz less suspicious,' said Netta. 'The more relaxed he is, the less chance there is that anyone will get hurt. I'll order a backup helicopter and then we'd better get moving!'

Zaphira looked at Anika and said seriously in Arabic, 'Don't. If you don't want to, don't! You have no responsibility for my hopeless family.'

Anika looked at Zaphira, and bit her lip. 'But this might save Ahmed's life,' she said.

Chapter 18   *Beach house*

Anika and Zaphira sat in the afternoon sunshine on two chairs with blue and white cushions. Between them was a small table with a jug of iced lemonade and glasses. They were on the front balcony of the beach house. Anika was trying to draw in a new notebook, but her hand wouldn't stop shaking. Zaphira was turning the pages of a magazine.

'This waiting is terrible,' said Anika in Arabic.

'Speak English,' said Zaphira.

Tall trees and dark bushes surrounded the house. The girls could see between the trees to the beach and the shining sea. The sun was still hot. Below the balcony, the swimming pool was bluer than the pale, misty sky. The policeman who had driven them here was now dressed in shorts. He was pretending to plant flowers by the garden fence to their left.

A car arrived at the back of the house. Doors banged. The girls checked their false hair and put on their sunglasses.

Voices sounded in the house. Then Nikos and Netta and four men appeared by the swimming pool. Nikos led them to a table in the shade on the other side of the pool. There were drinks and papers on it.

Zaphira and Anika watched as Maritz, Karimi and two men they didn't know sat at the table with Nikos. Karimi got up and went over to the gate in the fence between the garden and the beach.

'Those other two men must be Maritz's lawyer and the accountant,' whispered Zaphira.

Anika didn't answer. She could hardly breathe.

Netta was wearing a swimming costume and a beach dress. She smiled and chatted to the men.

Maritz said loudly to Nikos, 'Let's get on with it, Mr Bryant. I have other urgent business I need to deal with.'

Karimi came back, but didn't look at the others. He kept looking around, checking for anything suspicious.

Zaphira whispered to Anika, 'Maybe that's something to do with us, or Ahmed. He must know we've escaped.'

Anika's fingers let the pencil fall onto the notebook.

Netta offered Karimi a drink. He thanked her politely.

Then Netta said, 'I'll leave you gentlemen to your business.' She pointed to her 'daughters' up on the balcony. 'The girls and I are going out soon.'

The girls waved back lazily and nodded their heads. This was the agreed sign that the blond man was really Maritz.

Netta said goodbye to the men and walked into the house. Zaphira and Anika collected their things and went inside.

Their instructions were to go through the house to the back balcony and wait there. Zaphira stopped at the top of the stairs to listen. Anika went on into the back bedroom.

She walked through the bedroom and out onto the back balcony. It was shaded by a large tree. Maritz's car was parked below the balcony, next to the car the girls had come in with Netta, Nikos and the driver.

Anika was shaking violently. She whispered to herself, 'It's OK. We're going to get Maritz. It's OK. Calm down.' She went to sit on a chair under a low branch of the tree.

But as she sat down, her false hair caught on the branch of the tree, and lifted off her head. She grabbed it with her good hand and ran into the bedroom.

A voice outside behind her called in English, 'Hey! It's a set-up!'

Maritz had left his driver in the car and he had seen Anika's false hair come off.

Anika found herself at the top of the stairs watching Zaphira run down them.

Netta's voice cried out, 'Stop!'

There was a crash and a cry – a man's voice.

Netta called out, 'We got him!'

Anika ran through to the front balcony.

From there she could see Nikos pointing a gun at Maritz and the lawyer and the accountant. The police driver also had a gun pointed at the three men. They stood like statues between Nikos and the driver with their hands up. Papers were falling onto the ground and into the pool.

There was no sign of Karimi.

Nikos was saying, 'Malcolm Maritz, you are under arrest. Walk towards the house, please.'

The lawyer and the accountant seemed rooted to the ground. Maritz was looking around for Karimi. His face was unrecognisable, he was so furious.

From above, Anika suddenly saw Karimi. He was hiding in the bushes and moving towards the police driver.

She cried out in English, 'Be careful! There's Karimi!'

Karimi looked up, aimed at her, and fired.

Anika fell to the floor and lay still, but she realised she wasn't hit. She looked through the balcony rails and saw Maritz running towards the trees at the side of the house. Zaphira appeared in front of him and he ran into her.

'You?' he shouted. Just then, Netta ran round the corner of the house with a gun in her hands.

'Don't move or I'll fire!' she cried. Maritz stopped and turned to her. 'Into the house!' she ordered, the gun level with his stomach. They went in.

Karimi had made his way through the bushes and was now opening the gate onto the beach. Anika called out, 'Karimi is at the gate!' and hid behind one of the chairs.

The police driver and Zaphira both ran to the gate as Karimi opened it.

Karimi ran out onto the beach with the driver chasing him.

Anika could hear the helicopter in the distance. Nikos was pushing the accountant and the lawyer towards the house.

Zaphira picked up a fallen branch from one of the trees. She threw it hard at Karimi.

As it flew through the air, Karimi turned and shot at the police driver. At that moment, the wood hit Karimi in the face. He swore, but ran on.

The driver stopped running, holding his right arm. He moved his gun into his other hand and shouted, 'Stop or I'll fire!'

Zaphira set off after Karimi. He turned and shot again.

She ran on for a few steps. Then she fell in the sand.

Chapter 19   *Waiting room*

There were police guards on either side of the swing doors of the hospital waiting room and more outside. There was a row of empty chairs along the wall to the right. Anika was sitting on the one nearest the door. Nikos came in, talking on his phone.

He finished his call and put the phone in his pocket.

'How is Zaphira?' asked Anika.

'Not as bad as we thought,' he said. 'They're treating her now, sewing up where the bullet went through her leg. I understand she doesn't need an operation.'

'Thank God,' said Anika. 'There was a lot of blood. Did they catch Karimi?'

'He's here, in the hospital!' said Nikos, smiling down at her. 'A small bit of Zaphira's branch went into his right eye. They say he'll lose his sight in that eye.' He looked serious. 'The police driver's quite badly hurt, though.'

'Poor man,' said Anika quietly. 'It was my fault.'

'It was not!' said Nikos. 'Never believe that!'

'But if I had been more careful about my hair …'

Nikos sat down near her. 'They are hardened criminals. It could have been far worse. How's your shoulder?' he asked.

'A bit better,' said Anika. They both kept looking at the door. After a few moments, she added, 'And Maritz?'

'He's been taken across the road to the Interpol offices for questioning,' said Nikos.

'What about Ahmed?' she asked.

Before Nikos could answer, the doors swung open and Zaphira was pushed into the room in a wheelchair. The top of her right leg was heavily bandaged. The leg of her trousers had been cut off.

'How was it?' Anika asked in Arabic.

'They just sewed me up,' said Zaphira. 'No operation.' The man pushing her wheelchair stopped it beside Anika, put the brake on, and left.

'So,' said Anika with a tired grin. 'We'll be able to compare the sewing skills of our doctors, you and I.'

Zaphira nodded, but she didn't smile.

'Does it hurt?' asked Anika.

'Not now,' said Zaphira. 'But it will. The bullet went through the flesh and left a mess where it came out.'

'No basketball for a while for us, then,' said Anika.

'They told me Ahmed's woken up after his operation and will be fine,' said Zaphira in English. She turned to Nikos. 'Will they let us see him?' she asked.

'Netta asked me to arrange that,' Nikos answered. 'So Ahmed should be here soon. Afterwards, he'll be locked up until he leaves the country. He isn't helping us at all, you know. After he went to the police in Faliron, he hasn't said a word. Please try and persuade him to talk to us.'

The doors swung open again and a policeman in uniform with a gun on his belt came in. Behind him a nurse was helping a young man to walk. He had bandages around his head and chest. Another uniformed policeman followed them into the waiting room.

Zaphira leaned forward in her chair. 'Ahmed?' she said.

Anika stood up and went towards Ahmed.

The nurse led him to sit beside Zaphira. There were tears on his bruised cheeks, but no other expression on his face. He needed a shave.

Anika couldn't believe she was sitting next to Ahmed. She sat on his other side and stared at him. He smelled of hospitals and sweat.

He turned to Zaphira with dull eyes, like black stones. Then he looked down at his hands. Zaphira took one of his hands in hers and whispered something in Arabic to him. He didn't look up at her, but Anika saw his fingers tighten around Zaphira's.

They could hear loud voices in the corridor. Then a man shouted in English, 'The nurses told me she's here. She's my responsibility! You have to let me see her.'

The doors swung open. It was Karimi. He stood between the police guards. His clothes were very dirty and he had a white bandage over his right eye.

Before anyone could move, he ran towards Zaphira in her wheelchair. Anika saw with horror that he had Zaphira's knife in his hand.

Karimi was shouting in Arabic, 'Evil woman! Daughter of a dog! You have blinded me!' He raised his arm above Zaphira's face.

As Zaphira lifted her arms to protect herself, Ahmed stood up and threw himself with a cry across her wheelchair, covering her body with his.

The knife came down on Ahmed's chest, once, twice, three times.

The guards at the door rushed forward and grabbed Karimi. Nikos ran to Ahmed. He lifted him off Zaphira and laid him on the floor, shouting for help.

Blood was spreading across the white bandages around Ahmed's chest.

A male nurse hurried in. He said, 'Don't move him! I'll get help.' And he rushed out again.

'Help me out of this chair,' said Zaphira to Nikos.

Sitting on the floor beside Ahmed, she touched his unshaven cheek and held his hand. Anika just stared.

Karimi was shouting and fighting with the guards. One of them hit him hard on the chin. He fell to the floor, unconscious.

There was silence.

Ahmed looked up at Zaphira with a sad smile. He took a breath and coughed. More blood showed on the bandages, and a thin line of red ran out of the corner of his mouth.

'I knew, when I left the bomb under the car, that it was the end of my life,' he whispered slowly.

Anika suddenly realised that Ahmed was dying. She went and sat beside him and took his other hand.

Ahmed looked at her and whispered, 'Anika. So beautiful.'

Zaphira said, 'Stop talking now. We'll take you home and make you well.'

'Too late,' said Ahmed. His hold on Zaphira's hand tightened. His breath bubbled in his chest. 'They'll let Mum go now. Tell her I did something useful at last …'

Zaphira touched his hair. 'You saved my life,' she said. 'Thank you.'

'And tell her I love her,' whispered Ahmed.

The door opened with a bang and two male nurses came in, pushing a hospital bed on wheels. When they saw what was happening, they stood still and quiet.

Anika watched in horror as Ahmed fought to take a breath. He made a terrible sound in his throat. His head fell back, and his eyes went blank, staring at the ceiling.

'No!' cried Zaphira. 'No!' She turned to the nurses. 'Do something! Do something! You can't let him die!'

One of the nurses bent down and put his arm around Zaphira's shoulders. The other lifted Ahmed's fingers away from Zaphira's hand. They helped her back into her wheelchair. She rubbed the tears off her face impatiently, watching as the nurses lifted Ahmed's body onto the bed.

Karimi began to come round. The guards pulled him to his feet and held him between them. Zaphira moved the wheelchair until she was in front of Karimi.

'Where is the knife?' she asked in Arabic between her teeth.

Karimi looked disgusted. 'He's got it,' he said, pointing at one of his guards with his bruised chin.

'That knife is all I had left from my brother,' said Zaphira. 'And now you have murdered my cousin with it. You have dishonoured my brother's memory.'

'One day I will catch up with you,' Karimi said to her, 'and then you will see how it feels – an eye for an eye.'

Half standing in the wheelchair, Zaphira leaned close to Karimi. She said, 'If they don't hang you for murder, I will find you and blind you in the other eye too.'

The guards pulled Karimi through the doors.

The two nurses followed them out of the waiting room, pulling the bed behind them.

Anika stood beside Zaphira in her wheelchair, watching Ahmed's body disappear along the corridor.

Chapter 20 *Plane*

At the airport, the girls were shown into a large, empty room with no windows. Anika sat down on a plastic chair beside Zaphira.

'Was it just this morning that we were prisoners on Maritz's yacht?' she said.

Zaphira nodded. 'And now it's nearly midnight, and we're free and on our way home,' she said. 'And Karimi and Maritz are in prison. But Ahmed is dead.'

The girls sat in silence. Nikos had told them that this room was 'reserved for unwelcome guests' when he had left them there earlier. Their sports bags were on the floor beside them.

Anika bent down and took her notebook out of her bag. She sat with it unopened on her knees.

At last Zaphira said very quietly, 'It was better for Ahmed that he died now.'

Anika looked at her, and then down at the closed book.

Zaphira went on, 'Who knows what sentence the court would have given him? He's been saved all that.' She paused. 'Nikos told me that Ahmed had planned to rescue his mother from Karimi's men and then take her somewhere safe to start a new life.'

'So his mother's still being held?' said Anika.

'I suppose so,' said Zaphira. 'But Nikos said Interpol were looking for her.' She paused again. 'You see? Sometimes the worst does happen.'

'It hasn't happened for you and me,' said Anika. 'We may be wounded, but we're still alive.'

They were quiet again.

'Does your mum know we're coming home?' asked Anika.

Zaphira looked at the ceiling and said, 'I think I may have to move away from home.'

'Where will you go?' asked Anika.

'Perhaps Ahmed's mum would let me live with her – if they find her.' Anika had never heard Zaphira sound so sad.

'Where's that?' asked Anika.

'Near where you live.'

'You could come to my school,' said Anika with a smile.

'I hadn't thought about that,' said Zaphira.

'We can go to basketball training together.'

'I thought you might not see that as an advantage.' Zaphira was studying the bandage on her leg.

'Why?' asked Anika. 'Won't we go on being friends?'

'*Are* we friends?' asked Zaphira, looking up.

Anika looked into Zaphira's worried face. '*I* think so,' she said seriously. 'To me, a friend is someone you can depend on to do their best for you. You don't have to agree with them about everything, but you have to know you can trust them.' She paused, and then said, 'I think we have both proved that to be true.'

The door opened and Netta hurried in.

'Ah! You're still here,' she said in English. 'I just wanted to thank you both for helping us to get Malcolm Maritz and Sayid El-Karimi. And to tell you that we have found and freed Ahmed's mother, Mrs Bakkal, in Alexandria. She is not injured. The men who were holding her admitted sending the message that the DFP was responsible for the Qaitbay bomb. They were working for Karimi, and have been arrested.'

The girls looked at her in silence. 'You must be exhausted,' she went on. 'In a few days, we'll be in touch about when and where the trials will be held. You will be asked to give evidence, of course.'

'Yes,' said Anika. 'I suppose we will.'

'You have helped stop something very big and very ugly,' Netta went on. 'Maritz was sending weapons to at least three African countries. We've probably saved thousands of lives by stopping him.'

'Perhaps,' said Zaphira.

'And I've brought you your phone back, Anika,' said Netta. She took it out of her handbag. 'It works now.'

'Thank you,' said Anika. She turned it over in her hands. 'You found the pictures of Ahmed at Qaitbay.'

'Yes,' said Netta, nodding sadly. Then she held a small envelope out to Zaphira. 'The SIM card you took from the man in Alexandria led us to Mrs Bakkal,' she said. 'And this is your own.'

Zaphira took the envelope and put it in her sports bag.

The door opened again and two policemen came in. Netta stood up. 'They're ready for you on the plane,' she said. 'But first, I just want to say that you have both been extremely brave and strong. When I was your age, I could not have dealt with what you have dealt with in these last three days. I am very proud of you.'

Neither of the girls knew what to say to that, so they were silent.

One of the policemen came over and began to push Zaphira's wheelchair towards a door at the other end of the room. He said, 'Miss Bakkal, you'll have to go up in the lift to the back door of the plane.'

The other man said to Anika, 'Come with me, Miss Hakim. We'll go this way.'

Anika looked round desperately. Zaphira was disappearing out of the other door.

'It's OK,' said Netta kindly. 'You're going on the same plane. It's just you'll have to use the stairs at the front, and Zaphira will go in the lift at the back. Goodbye, and good luck,' she added.

Anika walked out into the dark with her guard. He left her at the bottom of the steps up to the plane. Light from the plane door streamed down towards her. She climbed the steps as if she were in a dream.

At the top, a flight attendant said, 'Good evening, Miss Hakim,' in Arabic, and stepped aside.

From behind the flight attendant, a man stepped forward.

It was Gamal. He took both of Anika's hands in his and said, 'Thank God you're safe at last, Anika.'

'Oh Gamal!' cried Anika.

Their tears fell on his shirt as he put his arms around her and said, 'I promise I will never be late again.'